NORMAL MODES OF MADNESS

NORMAL MODES
OF MADNESS

Hurdles in the Path to Growth

by

William F. Kraft, Ph.D.

ALBA · HOUSE   NEW · YORK

SOCIETY OF ST. PAUL, 2187 VICTORY BLVD., STATEN ISLAND, NEW YORK 10314

Library of Congress Cataloging in Publication Data

Kraft, William F., 1938-
  Normal modes of madness.

  Bibliography: p.
  1. Self-actualization (Psychology) 2. Social
psychiatry. 3. Psychology, Pathological. I. Title.
BF637.S4K72   158.1   78-3865
ISBN 0-8189-0369-4

*Produced in the United States of
America by the Fathers and Brothers of the
Society of St. Paul, 2187 Victory Boulevard,
Staten Island, New York, 10314, as part of their
communications apostolate.*

1 2 3 4 5 6 7 8 9 (Current Printing: first digit).

In Dedication
TO MY COMMUNITY.

Thanks

Thank you Vincent Bilotta and Suzanne McClintock, for your editing, suggestions, and support. Thanks are also offered to the silent workers: Alvira Boughan, Denise Krall and Susan O'Leary for their typing and retyping. Thanks to my clients, students, teachers, and children who taught me to appreciate and celebrate the sense and the apparent nonsense of everyday living. And thanks to Mom and Dad who taught me to see— and, to my wonderful weirdo—Pat.

Contents

NORMAL MODES OF MADNESS

CHAPTER ONE

Normal Madness

Imagine a flock of birds. You probably see them more or less in the same formation, on the same course, and flying in a certain direction. But if you look again, you might see a few "weird birds," not in formation. Like the flock, society has its weird birds who for various reasons move in directions that differ from the normal course—and, we often give these people who are out of formation labels—weird birds, funny birds, peculiar birds, tough birds, dumb birds, sick birds.

Weird birds are more or less deviant people who for various reasons neither live in normal formation nor take a normal course. Their experiences are deemed senseless, sick, stupid, pathetic, foreign, or perhaps eccentric. Their deviation may be considered senseless and therefore something to purge, embarrassing and therefore something to hide, disruptive and therefore something to control, or weird and therefore something to withdraw from. They are "them" who differ from "us." "We" (normals) usually see "them" as "them"—weird birds.

But instead of just focusing on them, let us look at the birds in formation—at ourselves. Let us honestly question ourselves. Is our formation perfect? Hardly. Are we moving in the best possible direction? Can our course be radically improved? What if we too are mad. Listen to some normal people—to some of us.

"Really, I have everything I've ever wanted. I have a dependable husband, two wonderful kids, a nice house, and the freedom and money to do anything I want. I belong to a couple of social groups, a spa, and I get around a good bit. Anyone would say I'm lucky and have it made.

"What do I really have made? Everybody thinks my marriage is great—and, it's not bad. But sometimes I get the feeling my husband and I were closer fifteen years ago. Is that the way it has to go? My kids are great, but they're in school now and they're finding their own way. And, they should. Social life? It's okay, but so much of it is the same old thing. It's like I try to be enthusiastic in a boring situation. Some people tell me I have to be liberated, but I don't feel unliberated. School? A new career? Different activities? Are these the answers? I don't know.

"Most everyone else looks and acts like they're happy. But I wonder how they really are. I suppose I look good too, but I don't always feel that way inside. I get along and have a good grip on things, but—there are buts. There's nothing I can pin-point. It's more a question of what's right, or that there should be more right, more of something. Eat, sleep, get married, raise kids, have fun, socialize, do all the normal things. Is that all there is to life?"

This 33-year-old woman has all the modern conveniences that facilitate contented living, and she has opportunities to achieve success. Still, she feels there should be more to her life, that something important is missing.

"I think I'm doing okay. My life is about as good or better than the next guy's. I have a steady job that pays the bills. I have a nice family. Like everyone, my wife and I argue, but things work out and we get along. Actually she's good with the kids and takes good care of the house.

"I like sports. I play golf, bowl, and watch most of the games on TV. And we take a vacation. We'll usually go with friends or relatives and sort of have a big family affair. We have pretty good times. The wives stick together and watch the kids, and we have a ball. Don't get me wrong. We help out. The women don't complain.

"I guess I'm happy. Why not? I have most of what I want, even more than I thought I'd ever get. I can't complain. But let's be honest; sometimes I wonder. Like I have twice as much as my father, but am I really happier? I wonder if there's more to life than a steady job, a wife, two kids, sports, a vacation, paying the bills, reading the newspaper, watching television, eating, drinking, and sleeping? Is there more? Sometimes I feel I was happier when we didn't have so much. I felt closer to my wife and I got a kick out of my kids. I don't know. I guess I should be satisfied. Why complain?"

This 42-year-old man has reached most of his goals and has gotten most of what he wanted. He is not abnormal, crazy, or weird, but he is a normal person who is accepted and usually liked. Yet sometimes he wonders if there is more to life than being content with what he has. He wonders if he could be happier and closer to his family. He wonders if something is missing in his life.

Listen to this young woman. "Everyone thinks I got my life together and that my future offers great possibilities. I can't disagree with them, at least in some ways. I have no serious problems. I suppose I'm a well-adjusted young woman. I graduated with A's, was active in school and community affairs, and I have an excellent scholarship to a top graduate school that almost guarantees me a successful career. So why am I not jumping for joy?

"Well, I look at my parents. They're normal people and well intentioned. Both mom and dad are very bright, highly successful, and on top of life. They look good, but I see what they're really like. I know they are in love, but I wonder how much they make love. They get along with each other, along with their silent fights; but warmth, closeness, and passion are missing. Sometimes I think their sex relations are performed out of duty or simply to relieve tensions. Is this what married life is all about? An insipid love that masks loneliness? A successful adjustment that hides alienation? If this is marriage, then I want no part of it.

"They go on several vacations every year, but do they really enjoy themselves and each other? They have so-called friends who play the same phoney games like talking all about their latest vacation. It seems that everyone talks about the proper things without truly listening. They periodically see relatives, but sometimes I think to prevent family war rather than to show concern. Sure, they're kind and polite to almost everyone, but actually they patronize people who are not in their class. They treat them as if they are unfortunate, inferior beings.

"My parents have everything they want. They're in control of life. No one would say they are unhealthy. Whether admired or envied, they are recognized as being on top. Is this the zenith of life? If so, I'd rather be a failure."

A 37-year-old woman: "It was difficult getting divorced. I loved my husband and maybe I still do. But we simply could not live together without slowly killing each other. We tried, but things didn't work out.

What do I do now? I have five kids to care for—and, that's not easy, especially without financial or personal support. Although it's very difficult, I'm satisfied that I made the right decision. When I think of how close I came to settling for being half of myself, I shudder. I gave up being a docile functionary—somebody to satisfy my husband's needs and someone to take care of the children and the house. I do feel I regained my dignity, but where do I go from here?

"I'm lonely. You can find a guy who will try to satisfy you for a night or so. And sometimes it's tempting. But I don't want to let myself be used anymore. And where is the man who wants to live permanently with a woman who has five kids and who refuses to be a servant? And what about my career? I'm luckier than a lot of women: I have a college degree. Or am I? I have a decent job, but I get paid much less than a man who does similar work. And my possibilities for advancement are really limited.

"What should I do? What can I do? Is this what life is all about? I get tired of fighting for my rights. My life is better than it was, but I get that gnawing feeling that there should be more."

These unmarried women know that the marital myth of complete happiness can often be a lie. They not only question marriage but also their present and future lives. Both have the courage to say "no" to marital charades, but they wonder how they can fully realize themselves—how they can be more than content. Although they have rejected a conventional way, they still feel that there should be more to life.

Listen to this 52-year-old minister, "Well, it's been 27 years. Where has the time gone? I look back and wonder what I have to show for it. I suppose I have ministered and administered well; at least, that's what people say. But I feel I missed so much. I entered the ministry to be a man of God—to proclaim His word. Have I really? My spiritual life, or the lack of it, haunts me. Though I have been successful, I find myself alone in a desert with nothing to eat but sand.

"Where is the enthusiasm I had when I was ordained? How did I lose God's presence? How can I heal without spirit? Sure, I know and have taught the texts and theories that deal with the presence of God in His absence. But have I lived them? It seems that I have been so busy practicing the ministry that I forgot to live a spiritual life.

"And there's my marriage—my wife and I. We were so much in love. Everyone, including us, thought that ours was the perfect marriage. Where has our love gone? Not that we don't love each other, but the issue is how much are we in love. Our children have left, and our nest is indeed empty. Funny, we have the situation that we initially wanted—to be just with each other, and now we don't know what to do with it. I must painfully ask what has been more important to me—my marriage or my ministry. Could there have been, can there be, a common ground? I only know that my spirit longs for love."

A 50-year-old nun has a similar story to tell. "Next year I am going to celebrate my silver jubilee—25 years as a professed religious. Instead I feel that I will be taking part in a funeral and that I am the corpse. Perhaps that's too strong, but that's how I feel all too often.

"I shudder when I think of the past. How I and most of us were treated by our community and priests. For instance, our living conditions were often inadequate and seldom as good as the priests; and the sudden changes in location and job made me seldom secure. The authority some of my superiors had and used was sick. But holy obedience made us do some crazy things. How would you like to be thrown into a classroom of 80 kids with little preparation. It took me 17 years via the summer school route to get my bachelor's degree. Sure, I get bitter, but what good does it do to be bitter? Besides, there were good things, good times, and good people. And God was there; otherwise, we would have never made it.

"And I must admit that I get angry when I see how the young sisters are coddled and catered to. It seems that they take us middle-agers for granted. I've been on one real vacation in my religious life, and they go on two a year. Community life? Ha, where is it? I've been so conditioned against particular friendships that I don't even know how to go about making a 'non-particular' one. Besides, I don't see many reaching out to me. Where's the justice? Where is love?

"But my main complaint is about me. I don't know what has happened to my spiritual life—my reason for being. Work, work, work—that's all I have heard and hear. What help do I get with my spiritual life? When do I have time and energy to pray? I committed myself forever to the religious life, but where is the vowed, communal life for God. At least in the bitter old days, we witnessed to Christ. Now we're just service people who work for less than others. What happened to that dream I had as a young girl—to serve and love God?"

Though these two people differ in the kind of ministry and communal lives they live, they are public people of God who share similar values and questions. These two persons committed themselves to serve God and to be witnesses to His love. They wonder if they have grown in the spirit of God as much and as well as they should or could have. They wonder about their concrete implementation of love in their community, their work, the world, and especially in their personal lives.

The sister feels anger and resentment toward many of her past and present situations, but she realizes that life is basically in her hands especially in her relationship with God. Though bitter, she yearns for a deeper and more fulfilling life. Likewise, the minister experiences the absence of God and desires His Holy Spirit. Though in the darkness of depression, he seeks the light of joy. Both people of God seek to live more integrally with people and God.

A 70-year-old man: "I've been retired for several years and I think that I've done quite a lot. I got to be president of our firm, traveled around the world, met important people, have an intelligent and attractive wife, good health, two kids, good investments, three houses, money, and an excellent pension. What more can a man ask for?

"We have a nice life. We spend the cold months in the South and travel back North for the summer. I play some golf, do some consulting, and watch my investments. Exciting, isn't it? Hell, whom am I trying to kid? I'm lonely. My wife goes one way and I go another, or we sit and stare. I feel bored, depressed, just kind of empty. I look back on my life and everything seems so great. I was a super success, got honors—everything everyone ever dreams of. So what! I still feel empty. What happened to my kids? I was so busy being a success that I missed them. Sure, I'd buy them presents, but I seldom enjoyed and had fun with them. I don't really know them and sometimes I think they don't love me. Anyhow, we're not close.

"Neither are my wife and I close. We love each other—what choice do we have? But our love is distant, too proper and adjusted. We operate together, but we don't really communicate. By communication I don't simply mean an exchange of information but more an understanding and appreciation of each other's feelings, views, values, and maybe to understand and accept our misunderstandings. It's not a true confession game, but a real union with—a sharing. Instead, we've learned to live together by staying out of each other's way. I get the feeling that I'm going to die without really loving."

All of these people are normal. They are basically adjusted, successful, and contented, they are not abnormally mad. They are more or less like most of us—the person down the street, a neighbor, a relative, you, me. Most of us are not abnormal—psychotic, criminal or weird, and we cope with life in acceptable and approved ways. Still, as these people, we may feel that something crucial is missing. Initially everything may seem alright, but a second and closer look uncovers feelings that question our normal lives. Below the surface of our personalities, we yearn for more than satisfaction, adjustment, and success. Perhaps in our most silent moments we hear a voice ask: "Isn't there more to life than this?"

What if we normals who are apparently adjusted and content are not necessarily living in the best possible way? Are the husband and wife, who operate well together but who do not understand and appreciate themselves and each other, living the best possible way? Are the married couples really happy, or are they playing charades of happiness? Are they growing older together in love? Or does their normal marriage mask a life of alienation? Do the unmarried people live life to the fullest? Are they happy with their lives? What does their loneliness say? Can the people of God say "yes" to their spiritual lives? What does their desert experience say? Can these people—and you and I—say "yes" to life when we die?

Although most of us are normal, we can deprive ourselves or be deprived of important and necessary experiences. To be sure, everyone is limited and anyone can be judged to be missing much of life. To say yes to one experience means saying no to many others. Still, we can too easily reject what is available to us. Instead of embracing life, we can hide and run from ourselves and others. In our mania to be normal, we can numb ourselves

and lose the spirit of living. To seek contentment, to be successful, to have more are meaningful and to a degree necessary. But
when we see such values as paramount, we become mad.

We become mad when we make an activity other than love as
our ultimate concern. Thus, a key dynamic is that spirituality is
repressed, forgotten, or minimized, for love is the life of the spirit.
In this context, spirituality refers to the art of maintaining and
promoting good and transrational experiences. Spirituality, for
instance, can include such experiences as meditation, contemplation, celebration, leisure, compassion, faith, hope, and above all:
love. Thus, normal madness may be an obstacle to and/or a rejection of spirituality.

First, let us wonder. How and why are some actions normal,
while others are not? Why is it so important to be normal? Is
it necessary to feel that something crucial is missing, that love is
mostly present in its absence, that there must be more to life than
this? Where is the spirit of our lives—the spirit that fosters on-
going meaning and integral living? Is normal behavior always
positive, good, or healthy? What does normality mean?

NORMAL LIVING

Most of us share certain values and standards that influence
and characterize our normal lives. For instance, a clear sign of
being normal is to function without any serious abnormalities,
like mental illness. The people next door are unlikely to hear
voices, think they are God, be unable to communicate, or be
immobilized by depression. Rather than being psychologically
unhealthy, they can probably cope with reality; they are normal—
like most of us. We assume, however, that since we are not unhealthy, we are healthy. Does preventing unhealthiness guarantee
healthiness? Not necessarily. A lack of unhealthiness means that
we are normal—not weird birds, but not necessarily healthy. Many
of us are neither healthy nor unhealthy. We are normal. Just
because we can cope well and are satisfied does not mean that we

are healthy. We will see that authentic health includes and goes beyond normal living. Healthiness explicitly or implicitly incorporates spirituality—the art of loving.

Nevertheless, to function according to norms makes sense—and is necessary. We can and must function, communicate, and work according to common standards; otherwise, we and society would dissipate. By accommodating ourselves to various people and situations, we prevent chronic disruption and maintain order. Work and communication can enable us to satisfy our needs and to build a better world. And most of us manage to deal with life's vicissitudes rather than feeling helpless or overwhelmed.

A key symptom of normality is to be "reasonably content." When content, we are apparently secure and satisfied. We have a good hold on life and can live without excessive worry. We probably have most of what we need, and being content we **are** basically satisfied. Satisfaction, a principle of normality, means that we make and get enough to live a relatively painless life. We satisfy our basic needs: we eat enough, sleep enough, have shelter, some self-esteem, and common security. We manage to maintain ourselves without persistent dangers and though we can become upset, we can usually return relatively quickly to our settled state of rest.

It is necessary that we gain satisfaction. If we are starving, it is usually difficult to do anything, and if we do not get enough support and love, we may doubt ourselves and others so much that we find it difficult to function without debilitating stress. So if we are not normal—if we do not satisfy our basic physical and psychological needs, we may die or be crippled physically and/or psychologically.

We have seen, however, that we can be securely satisfied and feel deprived. We can have a personal and professional vocation, cope with life's demands, have a hobby, socialize, be informed, watch television, eat, drink, defecate, and sleep. Although we may be adjusted and content, we may also feel that something important is missing in our lives.

Normality can mean satisfaction of needs and achievement of goals to the exclusion of spiritual growth. Without growing imperfectly in the perfection of love, life can be lost, violated, or destroyed. We can forget to nourish the spirit in our lives. When we only nourish our physical and rational dimensions, we starve our meta-physical and trans-rational selves and become spiritless people.

Another implicit norm of normal living is equality. Equality means that everybody should have the same opportunity to be like everybody else and to receive the same treatment. Equality also means that we are basically predictable and comprehensible. If everyone were totally unique, we would be total strangers to one another. For instance, community members usually expect to have the same opportunities and support as one another and feel that they can depend upon one another to act in certain ways. Equality supports and promotes necessary familiarity, predictability, and communication.

Normal also means we are able to adjust to most situations. We can act correctly at least insofar as we can give the minimum demanded in a situation. Instead of being overwhelmed by pressures, we can cope with a change, competition, and daily stress. For instance, though a sudden change in work location may cause stress, we can accommodate and deal rationally with upheaval. Or when a loved one dies, we soon return to our normal life. In spite of usual and unusual stresses, we manage to adjust.

Yet, how do we feel inside—what do we experience behind our normal behavior? Normality can mean to act "properly" no matter what you feel—adjust, cope, look good regardless of what you really experience. We can too easily numb feelings like anxiety, depression, and anger that may indict our mad lives. We can cover inner emptiness with signs of normality, success, activities, or things. Our lack of significant meaning can be hidden behind a front of false fulfillment. Experiences that are necessary for meaningful and healthy living can be submerged under the surface of normal adjustment.

Part of adjustment is the ability to compromise. We can give up or modify something to get something in return. We try to go half way instead of demanding that everything go our way. We learn that we must often accept others wishes to have them accept ours. We discover that community living is an imperfect struggle in perfection—a life that calls for at least compromise, acceptance, and civility. A life without compromise can be narcissistic.

Nevertheless, compromise can promote behavior that destroys authentic communication. Although we may be encouraged to express how we really feel, thoughts and feelings outside the confines of normal conduct may seldom be understood and rarely promoted. We can be open but only if we conduct ourselves in a normal and non-threatening way. We can face one another with masks of madness that give the illusion of true communication. Healthy communication promotes respectful sharing and understanding that promote honest and true experience rather than mere normal conduct. Communication in love may have to break through normal exchange to be the basis of healthy compromise—an inexhaustible process of giving and receiving.

Adjusted people are balanced. By compromise and control, we learn to keep on an even keel. Though we may have some highs and lows, we seldom go overboard. We may become very angry, but seldom do we maintain or increase our anger for a long time. When we feel anxious, we are apt to control our feelings via thinking, activity, or drugs. Or if we really feel high and giddy, we are likely to temper ourselves after awhile. We seldom act "crazy" for long periods of time; we are careful to stay on our rockers.

When we do conduct ourselves abnormally, our behavior may be just or unjust. For instance, extreme manifestation of hurt may be an attempt to elicit pity and comfort. Or hostile anger can be in service of control and manipulation. On the other hand, behavior that is beyond normal conduct and consequently judged as off balance or crazy may be justly significant. To scream in pain can mean that our life has to be changed. To shout in anger can give us the strength to affirm ourselves. Sometimes, abnormal behavior can be in service of health.

Spiritual structures and exercises that promote an on-going life of love are not necessarily socially reinforced. To reflect on scripture, to contemplate life, to do nothing, to be, to love may be accepted or tolerated, but they are not encouraged and taught as much as practical reading, analytic problem solving, doing something, having more, and work.

Thus, to live a spiritual life—to maintain and promote good and transrational experiences of which love is paramount—may be considered a bit different. To do nothing rather than something, to feast instead of eat, to be instead of do, to play instead of work, to contemplate instead of think, to love instead of cope may evince cultural, community, family, or neighborhood flack. Such behavior may intimidate, upset, or make the normal flock feel uneasy. Spirituality can evoke people's forgotten spirits.

Being normal, we function rationally. We can usually think things out and make decisions without much wasted time and energy. And our efficiency enables us to succeed at work and in everyday behavior. We try to know what is important, to set goals, to take the means to reach them, and eventually to acquire success. And those of us who are highly successful may feel that if something works it is justified, and when it does not work, it becomes inoperative. What is operative can become a criterion for normal activity.

Power is implied in being normal. We have the ability to adjust to reality. We can satisfy our needs and deal with people, along with maintaining a job and meeting life's demands. We are seldom overwhelmed or helpless, rather we can control and use life to achieve our goals. Unlike most of our abnormal brothers and sisters who are mainly powerless, we can cause change and influence others. Indeed, we vary in our degree of power, and some of us have much more than others. The work of a politician usually gives much power, and the role of a parent or teacher gives special power to influence children. Regardless of the degree and kind of power, however, we have sufficient power to cope adequately, to maintain ourselves, and to support the surrounding system.

We have sufficient strength to cope with and adjust to everyday living without excess. Normal competency means that we can take care of ourselves and that we can usually take some responsibility in relation to others—to meet life's demands, to cooperate with others, and to fit into society. Being able to seek and work with people gives satisfaction, success, and a certain kind of security.

Rationality, power, and competence are necessary for, but do not constitute, healthy living. The transrationality of mystery, paradox, and transcendence, the power of surrender and being with, and the competence of seeking permanent meaning in love are also essential parts of healthy living. To repress, forget, or minimize such spiritual values is the primary force in normal madness.

NORMAL MADNESS

"Normal madness" may sound contradictory, absurd, or mad to our normal ears. We usually think that normality and madness are totally different. Normality is accepted, expected, rewarded and promoted, and madness is rejected, suspected, punished and suppressed. Is madness necessarily abnormal, or can it be normal? What is madness?

Consider madness as being actively closed to realities that are necessary for healthy and holy living. Being mad, for whatever reasons, we say "no" to experiences that are essential for meaningful and integral living so that we fail to say "yes" to the fullest of being alive. We are off balance, out of touch, and absurd.

Two basic kinds of madness are proposed: normal (covert) and abnormal (overt). Normal madness is more hidden and subtle and less conspicuous and alarming than abnormal madness. Although abnormally mad people deviate from socially sanctioned norms, we normally mad people keep and promote the norms.

Think of abnormally mad people. Some, for instance, will not or cannot respond productively to available realities like social responsibilities and work. Their withdrawal from the normal world, however, can be both mad and meaningful. For instance, if we as parents demand love and then become cold and rigid when our children try to love, we violate them by putting them into double binds: We say love and don't love. The children can learn to distrust self and world, to be confused about the truth of reality, and to withdraw from personal and impersonal communication. Consequently, they may construct their own world—a private fantasy that gives some satisfaction with less interpersonal pain. What they experience, however, is rigidly limited so that, for example, they can neither work at a normal job nor deal adequately with people. Their freedom from the environment limits their freedom for success and enjoyment. They suffer too much and unnecessarily, and their pain is the price they pay for saying "no" to reality. Although their psychotic option may be a refusal to play mad games of normality, their refusal to respond to normal madness is a form of madness. A paradox of psychosis can be that the attempt to escape normal madness results in abnormal madness.

The madness of normality is a different way of saying "no" to reality. When we are normally mad, we can function within society; we can get along with people, adjust to situations, work, and contribute to society. We are not blatantly off balance or out of touch as abnormally mad people. Our pace is not as chaotic and primitive as a psychotic's; we are not displaced via social ostracization or institutionalization; and our lives are more easily understood and consistent than those of psychotics. We usually expect normal people (us) to act in certain ways, and we seldom disappoint one another. We usually show up for work, communicate sensibly, and take care of ourselves.

Still, we too can be mad if we neither live at our pace and with the rhythm of life nor find our true place in the world. When we compulsively strive to have as much or more than others and to be professionally and socially successful, we may live such a rapid and alienating pace that we miss essentials of life. We may find that playing with loved ones or enjoying a sunset have no place in our pace. We may discover late in life that our mania for having, depreciates our being—that our normal life leaves us unhappy. When our lives make no significant sense and exclude the deeper and lasting dimensions of self and others, we may be just as or more mad than abnormally mad people. If, for instance, we are too tired or too busy to love deeply, we may be mad. Although we may be very normal in our ability to cope and to achieve, we miss many opportunities to enjoy life. Although we may be admired for our work, we fail with our community. And though we may be content in that we have everything we want, our reluctance to wonder about and to celebrate life leaves us festering in emptiness.

We can be mad because we merely try to adjust and to maintain ourselves. Our mania for compromise maintains a static and bland balance that precludes and excludes an enthusiastic and spirited mode of living. Instead of living a life of love, we may take almost everyone and everything for granted or even use them exclusively for our own welfare. We can be satisfied but lack permanent meaning, experience pleasure and gain success but not happiness and love. In our search for contentment, life can pass us by. Specifically: we are mad when we repress, numb, and are estranged from experiences that make us wholly alive. To love as well as to work, to do nothing along with something, to contemplate in addition to thinking, to grow wholly rather than to cope fragmentally are necessary for healthy and happy living.

We can be conditioned to settle for less than is possible. We can learn to believe that certain experiences are not worth striving for or we can learn to minimize, repress, or take for granted experiences that are beyond the norms. In time, we can lose ourselves and can forget how to regain our whole selves. Forgotten is surrender to others—a life in love. Forgotten is the courage to move out of normal formation to celebrate instead of just coping with life. Forgotten is the ability to dance with life.

In our madness we do not become what we realistically can become. In only trying to maintain and adjust ourselves, we play safe. For instance, we may play a role of being happy and fulfilled usually to an audience whose applause reinforces our madness. The circular reinforcement of madness is maintained, strengthened, and sanctioned. "I'll pretend that you are happy and secure if you pretend that I am happy and secure, and we'll both pretend we are not pretending" is a covert and cohesive contract that can hide basic unhappiness and insecurity.

Our madness points to a subtle shallowness that can fester violently within us. Although we may be knowledgable about the latest techniques, we may have difficulty perceiving personal issues so that too often we have preplanned answers for the mystery of living. Suffering people who reach out to us may be treated as a problem to analyze and solve rather than a person to appreciate and care for. A dying person may be assessed in terms of needs and lack of acceptance but not compassionately embraced.

Our lack of aesthetic appreciation may also indicate our lack of depth. To enjoy a sunrise can be seen as a sentimental indulgence rather than as an enjoyable and healthy luxury. A conventional view is to take such natural events for granted and consequently miss them. A painting is to look at—not to experience. Art may be interesting or pleasant, but seldom an inexhaustible source of meaning.

Our mad life styles often restrict openness and enthusiasm. We can too easily adjust ourselves to a boring life, go through the motions of living, and lack a sense of celebration. Our lives can become too mundane, heavy, and lifeless. We can get caught and stuck in doing what everyone else is doing. For example, a simple task such as mowing a lawn may be approached as a thankless job to get done instead of enjoying the experience—to see color, to smell grass, maybe to feel and taste it, and to move with nature in non-linear ways. To be in awe of the sky and to experience the life of a tree are considered mystical nonsense. We would rather experience cutting grass as nothing but work.

We can sell ourselves far too short. In our mania to maintain ourselves, we can realize a small fraction of our potential. Seldom do we dream dreams we struggle to fulfill. Being content with contentment, we miss much of life.

When mad, we try to stand still. We are almost the same today as we were ten years ago. From a distance we might appear to have progressed, but from a closer perspective we are the same persons. We might be more informed but not wiser. We may be richer in things but not in spirit. We can get physically older and more socially successful and psychologically adept but fail to grow spiritually. Instead of being deeper in love, we may have learned to adjust to falling out of love. Rather than becoming more enthusiastic, we seem less happy than when we were younger. We look older and have a bit more, but our lives are more lifeless.

In madness we speak too much and listen too little. Since we too often fail to listen to ourselves and to others, insight and sharing are minimal. We can speak repetitively—a repetition in service of our own bias and insecurity, and we say little except that we want to maintain or strengthen our status quo. Perhaps we cannot listen because listening expands our views, broadens our personalities, and changes our speech.

Sometimes it seems that we have hearing impairments. We repeat the same stories regardless of protests of boredom. We seem to be unaware of others who are treated like non-responsive sounding boards. Silence and listening are aborted in service of verbal narcisism. When others speak, we respond cryptically, or not at all, and quickly return to our own interests. Rarely do we show a genuine interest in what others say and neither do we make concrete efforts to understand and appreciate their world.

When a group of us meet, our madness compounds and results in a chaos of monologues. Although some elderly people may seem to manifest similar behavior, brain damage is often, though not necessarily, the main cause. We can act as if we have brain damage.

Listening means to be quiet and to see another's viewpoint as he or she sees it. We listen when we partake of the world of others—when we appreciate what life really means to them. We try to suspend our judgment in order to understand, and understanding leads to creative talk—words that uncover, not cover, the truth. Instead of monologuing, we can dialogue—listen, understand, appreciate, speak, and share.

Normal madness also means that a sense of surprise in daily living is seldom perpetually present. Instead of experiencing new meaning, nothing much new is the normal route. Enjoying a shower, celebrating food, experiencing a walk are too absent. Being blind and bland, we tend to be equal in our lack of enthusiasm. The spirit of living becomes buried under convention.

Think of eating. We must eat to satisfy our needs; otherwise, we would die. Eating, however, can be more than normal need satisfaction. Instead of taking food for granted, eating can be feasting that opens new worlds of meaning. At the feast all the senses play in concert—to see, to listen, to smell, to taste and to feel the food and drink. The good things of God, earth, the sun, moon, rain, animals, vegetables and fruit, the farmers, producers and cooks, the skill, care and concern, the music, mood and decor, the past, present, and future, the drink, food and conversation, the pleasure, mirth and goodwill, the letting go, letting be and being with in companionship—they all come together for the feast.

Still, we often miss what is in front of us. We can forget that any meal, even a snack, can be at least a mini-feast. When we use food only to satisfy our basic needs, we are too normal and somewhat mad. In our pursuit of success we can pass over the richness of everyday living. Starving, we fail to appreciate life as a banquet.

Few of us live this kind of life exactly and constantly: Most of us try to live fully and are not entirely estranged from integral living. Although many of us may not realize ourselves as fully as we can, we do struggle for a good life—and, all of us should be more or less normal—to adjust and maintain ourselves. A main point, however, is that too many of us can see this kind of normality as our ultimate goal and consequently be normally mad.

NORMAL, MAD, GOOD, AND BAD

Most of us, more or less, are mad. The key phrase is "more or less"—how and to what degree does madness influence our lives. At one extreme we can have normally mad life styles that constantly move against the flow of happy living. Suffering for another's sake is nonsense, giving without getting is ridiculous, and loving for the sake of loving is absurd. We give only when it is satisfying, safe, and convenient. Although everything may be quite satisfactory, nothing really makes much sense. We may be rich in things, but poor in spirit. We can end up active but bored, content but empty, alive but dead.

On the other end of the continuum, we can be rarely mad. We may have mad tendencies in particular areas but basically struggle to lead good and happy lives. Although our mad moments impede integral living, we try to learn from our experience to become better. For instance, if I realize that I can be a workaholic, I may set structures that enable me to play and love. I may daily set aside time for my children and spouse and for play and solitude. These times are not fringe benefits but are considered just as or more important than work time. Actually, my tendencies to be a workaholic can help me to be a healthier and happier person.

Most of us fall somewhere in between these two poles. Our goal is not to reinforce a mode of normal madness, but to learn from madness. We can slide deeper into madness and out of health, or we can strive to grow deeper into health and out of madness. The degree of truth and honesty in our struggle makes life more or less meaningful, fulfilled, and happy.

Normally and abnormally mad people, us and them, can also be good or bad. Our modes of madness can be bad—that is, we can destroy life emergence. We can willfully exploit, manipulate, and generally make the lives of others miserable. We become hard, vicious, and bitter about life. Our lives become fraught with self-hatred and emptiness, and dignity and integrity are painfully absent.

We can lead bad lives by becoming increasingly self-centered. We may blame others for our own misery, try to make others feel bad, and basically hate ourselves and others. We are unhappy, empty, and bad. Since our style is to exploit and manipulate people to satisfy our own needs, people feel uncomfortable and cautious with us. We do not try to love. Instead of promoting life, we destroy life.

And we can be good. We can try to do the best we can for others—nor primarily for our own welfare but for the sake of others. And people usually respect us. It is possible for us to promote life's emergence and to live basically in peace and happiness. Despite everything, we can say that we have tried to do our best for ourselves and others. We can live in love.

Holiness, however, is not the same as healthiness. Though healthy persons are at least implicitly holy in that they promote their spiritual selves in living a life of love, unhealthy people can be holy. Although their unhealthiness means they are not living integrated lives, they accept their madness and strive to liberate themselves for others. For example, people who are unhealthily depressed can nevertheless lead good, spiritual lives. Though they are depressed, they can still struggle to do good for others, and their depression may even help them to be more thoughtful and compassionate. Their suffering may help them to appreciate and to bear the burdens of others, and ideally help them become wounded healers.

Some abnormal people can be better and happier than some normal people. A normally mad person who is bad is not as happy as a person who is unhealthy but good. The unfortunate occurance, however, is that abnormal madness is usually seen (by us) as complete nonsense and normality as the best way. Too seldom do we see abnormal people as possibly being happier or better than us. Yet, this is possible. Consider schizophrenic persons. To be sure, they suffer in not being able to cope normally, and their inner world can be confusing and painful. Yet, they can have a refreshing lack of pretense that can manifest dignity. Although they are not realizing themselves as fully as they could without being mad, they still can live with a sense of permanent meaning and enjoy life more than many of us.

Yet many mad people, both normal (us) and abnormal (them), are unhappy. We often live in a deceptive world that can pressure us to be caricatures of ourselves. For example, we can become bad disciples of powerism and try to control life so much that we fail to surrender to life's deeper meaning. Our manipulative approach blocks true listening and communication, and our exploitive ways hurt and alienate people. We can lack genuine respect and concern for others. When we are mad and bad, we violate life by impeding and destroying its emergence. Instead of celebrating life, we fight life. Instead of promoting life, we destroy life. Instead of enjoying life, we feel dead.

We can transcend madness and learn to become better persons. To transcend madness, we must see what is really happening, face to face, accept mad experiences, and listen to what they say about life. Once we come in touch with our mad experience, we begin to learn from it and to change life. If I am a workaholic, for example, I can admit that I am overworking and begin to make sense of my workism. I can set structures that allow and pressure me to play, love, and do "useless" things. In discovering that I overvalue possessions and minimize being, I can take care to recreate, enjoy, and be with others. Actually my madness can help me to respect, promote, and enjoy life.

We can constantly try to progress toward healthy living and honestly admit to our madness. Instead of trying to destroy, hurt, or manipulate people, we can perpetually strive to respect and care for them. Our lives can paradoxically embrace and transcend madness. Though madness can be an obstacle to a good life, madness in ourselves (and in others) can be a challenge to live a better life. Goodness, of itself, is no cure for madness; nevertheless, a good life can promote healthiness and give meaning to madness.

The hopeful paradox is that we can improve and better our lives both in spite of and because of our madness. For example, although it may be an obsessive compulsive person who must give a perfect performance to feel accepted, I can still care genuinely for others and do excellent work. I have to be aware of being too tight and narrow, and take care to be flexible and open. My obsessiveness can also help me be conscientious and motivate me to be spontaneous. If hostile, I can strive to be kind and considerate instead of mean and manipulative. Instead of hurting people, I can learn to help them, and by listening to and understanding my hostility, I can become sensitive to and compassionate with other hostile people. So instead of seeing others as enemies, I can come to embrace them as brothers and sisters. Or, even if I am schizophrenic and therefore cannot cope in competitive and functional situations, I can still play and celebrate, appreciate life like nature and animals, love people perhaps from afar, and nourish my spiritual dignity. Although a good and more or less mad life is not the ideal, it may be for some of us the most realistic way.

CHAPTER TWO

The Pressure to be Normally Mad

From a psychosocial perspective, normal behavior is what most of us can, should, and must do. For example, most of us can converse with other humans, but if we speak to the sky, we are usually considered abnormal. The majority of us share and promote certain behavior—in this case, speaking intelligibly to people. Since such behavior does not call for extraordinary performance, talent, or effort, it is in the grasp of almost everyone.

Normality also implies certain norms, rules, or standards for behavior. From early childhood we learn a sanctioned system of "shoulds and should nots" that make some behavior acceptable and other behavior unacceptable. A child learns that parents like and encourage certain behavior while they dislike and suppress other acts. Similarly, an adult learns that certain behavior, like being pleasant, acting intelligent, and looking and speaking "properly" evoke support, while other behavior like being angry, acting dumb, and looking and speaking crudely usually evokes negative responses.

This should and should-not process involves the pressure of expectation. A parent who expects a child to be normal is likely to repress and punish behavior incongruent with normal standards so that a child may have difficulty in being explicitly abnormal. We can learn to pretend that experiences outside the confines of normality do not exist, and consequently act as if so-called abnormal experiences do not happen. For instance, if people (especially parents) expect us to be only rational, our emotional and transrational experiences can be denied or dissociated. Or we can be programmed to behave as if we are only rational and/or emotional beings and consequently fail to promote spiritual epperiences.

Conversely, if a normal child is expected to be abnormal, like retarded, he or she could have serious problems in being equal and autonomous. For example, if family, relatives, neighbors, and teachers treat for whatever reasons a normal child as abnormal (retarded), the group can pressure the child to be what he or she is not—mentally retarded. Furthermore, social expectations are often personalized so that this child can learns to act retarded despite innate intelligence. Thus, we can learn to think and feel the opposite of what we really are and consequently deny part of ourselves.

The meaning of norms can depend upon a particular viewpoint, such as in theology, psychiatry, law, and technology, and these views can also conflict with one another. For example, a psychotherapist might consider a client's search for religious experience a symptom of immaturity or simply not a relevant issue in therapy; whereas, a spiritual counselor will probably consider this spiritual search as essential to healthy living. A technologist might say one's main value is usefulness, but an artist might see a person's uselessness as the main value.

Normality can also differ cross-culturally. Certain sects and societies revere persons who hear voices, but in most parts of the world they would be hospitalized. A United States norm is that men rarely get physically or spiritually close with one another, whereas in other cultures closeness is normal. What is normal to one can be abnormal to another. Our specific concern, however, is the meaning of normality in daily living here—neither in other cultures nor from specialized fields.

Unlike abnormality, normality also incorporates a "must." Normality is sanctioned: When we act normally, we are rewarded and when we deviate from the norm, we are punished. Norms are social expectations that pressure us (via sanctions) to act in certain ways—normal ways. For instance, when we break the rules of expected behavior, we can be punished or we can feel guilty (self-punishment), or both. And if we highly disrupt the lives of others, we may be socially ostracized; if we persist in our abnormal dialogue, we may be put in a mental institution.

Picture a herd of cattle. Staying within certain confines, the herd satisfies its needs and seems content. Straying cattle are unacceptable, and cowhands force them back into formation or sometimes they are left alone. But if the mavericks become too troublesome, they are punished, put in another herd, or slaughtered. Similar to the herd, we can live to maintain ourselves while being pressured to act in certain ways. Some people, however, may move out of formation and deviate from a norm. If these people refuse or cannot conform, they are labeled to signify their lack of normality and are seen as peculiar and perhaps forgotten. If these human mavericks disrupt normal lives, they may be punished (personally and socially), put in another herd (institutionalized or they enter a different community), or slaughtered (physically, psychologically, or spiritually).

Human mavericks are persons who are more or less out of normal formation and who deviate in healthy or unhealthy, legal or illegal ways from socially accepted and sanctioned norms. Frequently, extremely abnormal people, especially psychotic persons who are ostracized in institutions, are anomalies and often unsettling to normal people or society. "That just doesn't make sense;" "That's crazy;" or "That's too much" are common phrases that refer to such abnormal behavior. Since we normal people often assume that psychotic behavior makes little sense and cannot be more meaningful than normal behavior, such abnormal behavior is often denied, destroyed, or at least controlled.

Along with maintaining themselves, healthy people grow in integrity—which includes spirituality. Along with satisfaction and success, they grow in permanent fulfillment, and along with emotionality and rationality, they promote transrational experience. Rather than the bad, the good is chosen and promoted. No matter what, love is paramount. Their lives may be different.

Religious persons who take permanent vows of obedience, poverty, and chastity can also threaten and indict our normal lives. People who freely choose to be celibate can make us wonder about our sex lives. We can consider them naive or irrelevant because they question us in crucially relevant ways; we may feel uncomfortable and embarrassed in their presence because they may see through our normal masks of madness. Or we may pressure them to be "one of us"—to minimize "their" values and to reinforce "ours"—and, too often an individual may succumb to this pressure.

We often tolerate abnormal people unless they become disruptive, troublesome, and in general upset our normal functioning. For example, although mentally retarded persons are considered abnormal, they may be accepted or tolerated as long as they are "harmless" and not intrusive. When they disrupt normal people (us), perhaps playing with our children, different actions may be taken. The parents may be told that their mentally retarded children must be watched and confined; otherwise, they may be institutionalized.

Maybe they (abnormals of whatever kind) intimidate us (normals). Maybe their abnormality stirs the abnormality hidden within ourselves.

A crooked business executive, who may be more criminal than a petty thief is often left alone—partly because he does not directly impede our normal functioning (and because of his power and wealth). Since the petty thief is more directly intrusive, he is more likely to be punished and ostracized.

Some normal people need abnormal people. "We" need "them" —the mentally ill, the mentally retarded, criminals, and more subtly semi-abnormal people. Consider, for instance, that too many of us identify ourselves in terms of what we are not—not Black, non-Christian, not foreign, not mentally ill, not mentally retarded, not a convicted criminal or not bad, not abnormal. But we seldom ask ourselves the question: What does it mean to be white, Christian, American, healthy, intellectually competent, law abiding, good, or normal—or, what does it mean to be Black, non-Christian, foreign, mentally ill, mentally retarded, criminal, bad, or abnormal?

Although hypernormal living is not abnormal, it is mad. Unlike abnormal madness, it is insidious, pretentious, and illusory, is often supported and promoted, and is sometimes esteemed and striven for. Like all madness, normal madness makes sense and nonsense. We normally mad people have the power to maintain ourselves, to cope with and control life, and to acquire some social acceptance. Not to be abnormal can give us feelings of superiority and power. To be normal is to be right. We question not only these and other assumptions about abnormality but also propose that we normal people *can* be more mad and bad than abnormal people. We can hold ourselves back from being what we can become. Instead of discovering, we can learn to cover fulfilling and lasting experiences.

CULTURAL MADNESS

We have indicated how our culture can support and promote normal madness. Societal sanctions can keep us in mad formation, and many of us can be unaware of how much and in what ways culture can influence us. (In fact, our lack of awareness can be a mad cultural value.) We can accept, support, and follow values instead of questioning them. And if some cultural values are mad, then it behooves us to be aware of them so we can deviate from, circumvent, or transcend them.

We have also seen that society has the power to safeguard and enforce its norms and values. When we transgress cultural norms, we are usually more or less punished and as we have seen, if we disrupt people too much, we can be punished. For example, if I am mentally ill or said to be so, I may be accepted in a particular sub-culture or family, but seldom does society as a whole accept me. I can pay a social price for being mentally ill—often institutionalization.

Cultural values are mad when they induce and seduce us to live empty and boring lives. These values pressure us to be normally mad—to be much less than we really can be. They dovetail with, promote, and sanction personal and interpersonal modes of madness. The intent is not to imply that all cultural values are mad, but to explicate and analyze a few of the many conventional assumptions of the American myth that can have insidiously mad effects on us. Mad values like racism, ageism, and militarism will not be explicitly discussed because they have been analyzed in other works. The proposal is that certain sanctioned, propagandized, and esteemed cultural values can impede rather than promote healthy and happy living.

High in the United States heirarchy of values are pleasure, satisfaction, and contentment—criteria for normality. It has been shown that these experiences are necessary for normal and healthy living but when they minimize other necessary experiences, normal madness results. When totalized, these values exclude other values that may incorporate pain, dislike, or uneasiness that may be necessary for healthy living.

In this context, pleasure refers to a state of balance or homeostasis and to a lack of pain and tension. Societal values are heavily implemented in the marketing and advertising worlds and can promote and propagandize this pleasure principle. For example, little if any sense is made of the probable anxiety and loneliness in the crisis of young adulthood. If we are programmed to seek only pleasure, we can feel guilty about or try to escape the pain of becoming mature. Although we are more than pleasure seekers, we can seek too much pleasure. For instance, we can assume that pain should be tolerated, be ameliorated, or be gotten rid of as soon as possible and exclude the possibility of suffering in service of growth. We can judge pain as necessarily indicative of negative processes, and consequently feel threatened, repress the experience, or escape from or numb ourselves via drugs, sex, or work.

Although pain can be indicative of unhealthiness, physical, psychological, and spiritual pain can also be necessary and indicative of healthy processes like birth, learning, dying, and re-birth.

Satisfaction and contentment are also culturally supported and promoted. Satisfaction literally means to "make enough"—to get enough food, to get enough sleep. It seems as if we are programmed to feel that we have "holes" that we constantly try to fill. The main difficulty is that our holes are never completely and forever filled; they constantly reappear. And as we grow older, we become less satisfied no matter how much we have, and eventually dissatisfaction overwhelms our lives of satisfaction.

Many of us are culturally programmed to think that being satisfied is the answer to life. To vow a life of poverty or to fast for spiritual reasons is considered unusual. Lacking an abundance of food, modern appliances, or recreational facilities carry the cultural implications of failure and unhappiness. We cannot understand how some people or nations can lack some of the basic satisfactions and still be happy—how poor people who are somewhat unsatisfied can be happier than rich people who are totally satisfied.

The cultural message is that constant satisfaction leads to contentment. The goal is: "to be filled up." To say that you are reasonably content means that you have held on to a pretty good life and to be completely content means that you have it made. Contentment can mean that you have everything that you basically want, that there is nothing left, that there is a "period" to life.

Pleasure, satisfaction, and contentment as ultimate motivations and goals lead to stagnation and shallowness —to normal madness. Joy, wonder, and growth can be absent. The culture can pressure us to become bored with pleasure and meaningless in contentment.

Rationality is one of our most esteemed cultural values. To be rational includes being a clear thinker, a sharp decision maker, to articulate clearly, to handle things properly, and to accommodate to reality. Rationality, however, can be absolutized and change to rationalism. We can be programmed to make rational sense of everything and to approach life only as a series of problems that can be broken down into solvable issues. Our goal is to cope with, explain, and control reality—to have everything in hand and to be able to use things productively. Pushing the right button makes life run properly, and when life becomes inoperative, a new method of operation is sought.

A culture built upon rationalism is mainly impersonal and abstract, void of warmth and intimacy. Although we may express and act on feelings, seldom is such behavior judged to be as proper or valid as rational behavior. Feelings are judged to be too irrational and ambiguous to trust and consequently are rationally constricted and controlled. And though our behavior may be covertly motivated by non-rational experiences, our action is overtly rational so that rationality can be the means to achieve irrational goals.

Although we can become irritated and "lose our temper," we usually keep our feelings in check. We can live from the neck up —out of our minds, and in a real sense we are out of our minds. Our cultural push toward rationality particularly encourages and sanctions modes of normal madness like powerism, thinkism, and interpersonal phoniness.

An overemphasis on rationality also impedes and can exclude transrational experiences—those that involve the mysterious and paradoxical, the concrete and transcendent, and the clear and ambiguous. Experiences like contemplation, compassion, and celebration have no place in the house of rationalism. And love, the paramount force of spirituality and healthiness, can be repressed, impeded, minimized, or at least made secondary, leaving emotional and devotional voids.

To be sure, transrational and rational processes can function harmoniously. For instance, we can rationally structure life so that transrational experiences are more likely to occur. We can implement via rationality our spiritual insights. And we can permeate our rational operations with spirit so that all our behavior is in some way a manifestation of love. The lethal danger, however, occurs when rationality is judged to be the ultimate means to and criterion of truth. Then, rationality becomes rationalism and other non-rational experiences are minimized, repressed, or destroyed.

Taking a rationalistic approach, we seldom see beyond the surface, for we experience only what our rational categories allow us to see. For instance, instead of being an inexhaustible source of meaning, a tree is simply "a tree" that we pass by, cut down, or use. Life is forced to be clear, controlled, and predictable. We can delude ourselves into thinking that we have power over everything—that nothing is beyond our control. Since our society supports and promotes rationality much more than transrationality, we can too easily forget spirituality and become advocates of rationalism.

Closely related to a rationalistic approach is the culture's overemphasis on specialized information. Since being totally informed or competent in one area can be very difficult, we often specialize. We can strive to know the most about the least. And some of us may even try to be informed in many areas so we try to read everything in sight and listen to anything said. To be informed is rewarded and to be highly informed is admired though there may be little depth. For example, a teacher who can articulate the latest techniques and curriculum models (but who fails at teaching) is usually advanced, applauded, and rewarded more than the teacher who quietly and daily inspires and educates students. We can spend an enormous amount of time and energy becoming highly informed about life but enjoy little of it.

The push for technological knowledge and know-how can also pressure and influence us. And absolutizing technology leads to technocracy, maximizing methodology and means-centeredness. Everything must be efficient and work well, but "for what" is seldom asked. Thus, students can learn better ways to read and teachers better ways to teach, but what and why to read and who teaches are not equally valued and explored.

Technocratic madness may also be found in corporate industry and institutions where workers must be hyper-rational, informed, and technical. As workers we may perform a function that somehow contributes to the total but unseen product; our skill is seen as necessary to maintain and promote the efficiency, productivity, and power of the technostructure. Too few of us, however, participate in and appreciate the whole process, and personal satisfaction and creativity are often nill. Following this technocratic madness, we can become rich and skilled dolts.

Or we may abdicate the responsibility of becoming whole persons by hiding in the haven of the corporate structure. We find our identity in serving the corporation that rewards us for loyal and productive service. In projecting the corporation as a superhuman parent, we can maintain an immature existence and gain financial success and social esteem. Experiences like love and play and people like family and friends are secondary to and often sacrificed for the technocratic system.

Where and how does spirituality fit in a technocratic world? Without spirituality, society fails to grow as a community and the culture dies.

Our culture also esteems accommodation, often at the expense of other important experiences. To be successful, we learn to cope with reality efficiently and productively, and if we are really skilled, we have contingency plans in case something unexpected occurs. Rather than being open to, wondering about, and enjoying the mystery of living, our goal is to have plans for the unexpected so that we can accommodate ourselves to anything. Although accommodation is necessary, mere accommodation is an affirmation and reinforcement of madness. Never really saying yes or no—never taking a stand other than accommodating oneself—can be a precariously mad course. We can be "madly flexible"—ready to play any game, to tolerate anything, to look the other way, to bend and give up principles. Not to accommodate—to disagree, break down, break through, to transcend—can be abnormal.

Accommodation is often in service of and congruent with competition—another culturally esteemed value. Our culture stresses the importance of competing to succeed financially and socially. As young children we may soon discover that we must compete for attention in the home or that with peers we are pressured to compete to see who is the toughest, brightest, funniest—the "best." Upon entering school, we may quickly learn that competition is an essential element of education. We can see that our success is often at the expense of others' failures. Perhaps in college this competitive battle becomes most lethal, and in some areas of higher education any grade less than an A provokes anxious feelings of failure. Certainly competition can be healthy in promoting better performance and in engendering fun. Constantly playing with inferior players eventually harms one's own game and results in boredom, and competition at work can evoke our best. But when one person's success means failure in others and when competition excludes respect, then resentment and alienation result. Cold competition, without care, is mad.

Separating the sexes and making one sex more important or superior than the other sex is also a cultural value. An analysis of the history and dynamics of sexism has been done in other works and is not within the scope of this book. The primary concern is seeing sexism as a mode of cultural madness. For instance, over-emphasizing the male sexual modality and impeding the female one makes for a one-sided and weak culture. Specifically: to minimize the potentialities and contributions of women is self-destructive. United States culture prizes rationality, power, and other similar characteristics that have been falsely attributed to men more than to women. And qualities like tenderness, gentleness, and warmth and experiences like love, compassion, and intuition have been falsely attributed to women more than to men. Such sex role dissociation is mad.

Psychologically, over-emphasized values often indicate the opposite realities. In this case, men frequently over-emphasize the so-called masculine activities like physical and social power to compensate for tenuous feelings about true male identity. Men may dominate women because they cannot risk letting go and being with women. These madmen feel that the best defense is an aggressive offense that hides their precarious stand and fear of women. (Many women spontaneously know and use this.) Being intimidated by women and dreading their own bisexuality, men can try to repress, minimize, and exploit women. This masculine powerism, however, promotes an illusion of personal power that leads to a fragmented and shallow life.

Certainly, women should have the opportunity, if they desire, to be significant persons in society at large; however, they should also have the opportunity and support to be persons of worth anywhere. In justice, women and men should have a free choice of roles. But it is normal in Western civilization, especially for men, to consider the home or community as a feeding spot, resting place, and source of secondary meaning instead of as the dwelling place of primary meaning. Primary community can afford more opportunities than "the world" to go beyond normal madness.

Consider that cultural criteria for happy and successful living can be much more masculine than feminine. For instance, the standards for mental health and the criteria for judging mental illness tend to be masculine. Since few models of mental health are created for or by women, women can be forced to conform to sexist standards that constitute mad models of mental health. And since most doctors are men, women can too easily be manipulated or minimized.

Part of the madness is that women in certain areas do or can have more power and influence than men. For instance, women usually have a significant influence on children and consequently on the future of children and of society. Still, society's superstructure is highly masculine, and though nurtured mainly by women, a child can later minimize or reject the female's equality, and the consequent confusion can be traumatic and destructive.

Although the double standards in labor, politics, and society are notoriously unjust, more subtle forces may exist.

Some women can practice sexism by emulating the very process they hate. When equality means being the same as men—like workistic, poweristic, thinkistic—normally mad, then women may try to be as mad as men. But there are advantages to such madness such as social affirmation and economic and political power. Too many women, including feminists, minimize their own personal power within themselves and maximize the masculine power "out there." Selling themselves short, women can play into sexist hands. Men are willing to listen and to give freedom, for this means that they (men) are in control. Since the power of women as persons can intimidate men, men are glad when women remain docile or fight for "masculine power." Instead of being mad, women can be challenged to help men become more integral persons. Women, however, too often minimize their spiritual power and let themselves be overwhelmed by, or they join, the madness of sexism. The power of love ultimately has infinitely more power than sexism or any other mode of normal madness.

Another symptom of cultural madness is that success in our Western culture tends to be based more on what we have than on what we are. Madly enough, our possessions can give us a sense of security. Having two (houses, cars, children, televisions, dogs) instead of one are indications of success. Having more and more is a mad measure of happiness. We can be programmed to think that having a lot of things, friends, knowledge, and success guarantees a life of quality. Simply to watch a sunset, to listen to a symphony, to be alone, or to do nothing are seen as wastes of time. Or these kinds of activities are used as rewards instead of being necessary ways of living.

A sign of this madness can occur when we have the chance to increase our salary at the expense of uprooting and enjoying less time with our family. We usually choose money. We may rationalize our decision by saying that we can give our family more and deny that our family would rather have our presence than our things. Keeping up with neighbors can also be a sign of this game—judging one another on the basis of how much we have. To have an old car is frowned upon even though the car functions well. To live in the city may indicate less success as contrasted with moving "up" to the suburbs where a "better life" is offered. Certainly suburban living is not necessarily a sign of madness, but to assume that a particular place increases happiness, is mad.

We can easily be pragmatically strangled by our material success. For instance, the more we have, the more time and energy we must spend to service what we have, and the more we must get because there is always someone else who has more. To value and promote having over being is a sure way to violate life. And since "havism" usually takes money, and money takes work, the cultural value of having can easily pressure us to be workaholics.

Thus, a spiritual value like poverty—a virtue that promotes being over having, may seem rather stupid or senseless. Poverty is not the same as being poor, though giving up things or using things to celebrate being can have a witness value. Not having an excess of things, food, success, or whatever can liberate us for spiritual living. A key is that having should be in service of being, and being with, especially in love, is the most important mode of living.

Another questionable value is that the more formal education we have the better we are, and the more and higher degrees we have the happier and more successful we will be. Still, we can challenge these assumptions. We can wonder if it is necessary to have a college degree, let alone a graduate degree, to achieve inner and outer success and security. Although "havism" insures normality, it impedes and can destroy healthiness.

Cultural madness can lead to personal homogenization: the push to make everyone equal and the same. For example, the movement to lead everyone into the higher education process can dangerously confuse personal worth with job description, and it can militate against healthy pluralism that promotes different values and creative ways of thinking and living. For instance, instead of promoting critical and creative students, schools can level students into a homogeneous group of informed and dependent people.

The point is that everyone is unique. We are equal as human beings, but our thoughts, feelings, values, and lives differ. Instead of being suppressed and leveled, our differences ought to be promoted so we can be creatively together and at least keep one another honest. Stamping out duplicates produces an efficiently dead society, and promoting only normality is fatal to the culture.

We can see that madness is not simply in our hands. Although our culture is not entirely mad, important parts can promote personal and interpersonal modes of madness. Cultural modes of madness can be constantly proliferated consciously and subliminally. Political and cultural propaganda can create images that do not exist and make untrue stories believable. Magazines and newspapers can sell having at the expense of being and information at the expense of wisdom. Television and radio can constantly reinforce the messages of pleasure exclusive of permanent fulfillment and contentment exclusive of perpetual becoming. Education can reinforce hostile competition, passive accommodation, and insipid homogeneity. The cultural forces of madness can so permeate us that our lives become difficult even when we are aware of these forces.

Still, since society is not only influenced by culture but also makes culture, we can change the culture—make it more or less mad or healthy. An individual must start with self: recognize madness, combat its negative influence, and live a healthy life. Then, we can begin to help others. To do this, however, we must have the humility to be normal and the pride to be abnormal, to transcend normal madness by going beyond its false promises of fulfillment to where permanent meaning lies.

CHAPTER THREE

Mad Modes of Living

"I love my dad, but I don't feel I really know him. How can I? I don't see him very often. He leaves early in the morning and comes home late at night. And if he's not working weekends, he's probably playing golf. Even when he's at home, he's usually working or reading. Anyhow, he never seems to have time to spend with me.

"I can remember when I was little. I think I wondered if I had a father. He always seemed to be away on trips. And did we move! Just when we started to settle in a place, dad was asked to relocate. Dad asked us and of course, we moved. Why? Dad would say it was the only way he could advance in the company, and he'd tell us he worked so much because he loved us. He can't understand that I'd like less money and more of him. Sometimes I feel he loves his work more than he loves me. Certainly his work is more important."

This seventeen-year-old is protesting against a normal mode of madness—workism. In our context, an "ism" is a normal activity or attitude taken to such an extreme that it minimizes, represses, or excludes other significant experiences. The young woman's father makes work his paramount value so that everything else, including her, is secondary to or in service of work. Although he may deny that work is more important than his daughter, his behavior tells a different story.

Normal and mad modes of living make sense and nonsense. Our primary gain is to be hypernormal so that competency, adjustment, contentment, security, power, possessions, success, and a lack of unhealthiness are primary goals, besides acquiring secondary gains like recognition and affirmation from community and society. In our attempt to gain success and security, however, we can progressively alienate ourselves from others and eventually from ourselves.

Many factors influence our lives—especially values, goals, needs, heredity, and present and past environments. A key factor is our heirarchy of values. In living a normally mad life, our highest values and consequent behavior center around and are in service of mere normality.

Theoretically, almost any activity can be used as our ultimate concern so that it permeates and directs our life. The following "isms" or life styles are normal: They are socially sanctioned, supported, and promoted—and, they are mad. The selection of the modes of madness is based on their significance, frequency, and insidiousness. Although only some are discussed, other forms of madness can be understood in the light of the theory and following examples.

WORKISM

One of our most common and sanctioned modes of normal madness is workism. Workism occurs when work is our paramount lived value so that other activities and persons are secondary to work. Life is seen in light of work and our worth really comes from work. When working, we feel satisfied, content, worthwhile, and secure, and while "not working," we feel more or less dissatisfied, restless, invaluable, and ill-at-ease.

Indeed, work is important and in many ways work is essential, for life would dissipate without work. Perhaps work can be secondary, which means that it is more important than anything except that which is primary. But when work is made primary by a replacement for love, then workism or normal madness results.

If I am a workaholic, I try to take a work approach in most

areas. I find that I cannot stand to have time on my hands, and when I have spare time, I search for work. The same is true in leisure time activities: I am apt to read only to be informed, play cards with intensive competition, take a vacation to recuperate for work, and see play in itself as a waste of time. In sexuality, I may use sex as a relief from work, have sex in an efficient and technical way, or be too tired to love. My work-world can spread like a cancer that destroys experiences of play, beauty, and being.

Our culture's technocracy and thrust toward production and ownership promotes workism, for our success is often judged on what we own and can produce, not on who we are—and, what we have, highly depends on financial status which usually depends on work. Furthermore, good workers are adjusted and efficient persons who strive for success. The more successful we become, the more admiration, praise, and status we usually receive. Workaholics can be seen as models of success.

If I am an advocate of workism, I am not punished; on the contrary, I am rewarded economically and/or socially. People, especially those outside my immediate community, usually admire me for my efficiency, productivity, and success, and they may encourage me to succeed even more. Still, my normal life is mad because I minimize significant realities like family and community and experiences like celebration, play, and meditation. My absolute normality actually violates my personal growth.

As a professional workaholic, I can easily hide behind my professionalism and show credentials instead of myself. I may speak seriously about pragmatic and technical issues but minimize the value of nonsense and common sense. Furthermore, people may promote my madness by expecting me to act as a professional at all times. Think of a physician at a social gathering. Many people probably treat him with respect or caution, in any case—special, and they may be shocked or surprised to see him act unconventionally or even spontaneously. In turn, the physician may behave in a properly controlled and dignified way so that horseplay or kidding are simply absent. Most people expect

him to behave as "a doctor," and he may meet and reinforce
their expectations by being stuffy, distant, and cold.

I can be conditioned to use work to be hypernormal—to be
a workaholic. If I am economically poor, I may taste pleasure
and seek more, and under the influence of mass media assimilate
questionable symbols of a hyper-normal living. I can be led to
believe that success lies in having things instead of really living
life or in a fast car rather than a slow walk.

If I am a young adult who comes from a normal situation
that has maintained and satisfied me, I can take a comfortable
life for granted. Since I may be too content and have almost
every "thing," I might try to make my work more meaningful.
A tendency, however, is to work in service of life while in
school and for a few years after graduation, but eventually succumb to some degree of workism—to see life in service of work.
For instance, if I am a young married professional, I may practice in a rural area and spend and enjoy time with my family.
Later, under the pressures of children, bills, and cultural expectations to succeed, I may change my style of living and become a
workaholic. Or as a young religious or minister, I may structure
my life in ways that promote spiritual growth. But under the
pressure of workism, I may eventually forget to nourish myself
spiritually and settle for much less than is possible. Actually, my
original commitment to the spiritual life can be weakened and
perhaps lost.

Workism may be more understandable if I am middle aged or
older. Since I am likely to have come from a poorer environment
than younger people and have probably lived through the throes
of an economic depression, maintaining myself can be paramount.
If I was not sure of my next meal, I may look at money differently than a person who always took food for granted. A seventy-
two-year-old retired workaholic said: "When I got my first job
at thirteen, my life changed. Though I always worked hard and
long around the house, now I got paid. My job gave me a sense
of confidence and freedom that I never even dreamed of before.

The money enabled me to buy a second pair of shoes or buy a book. I started to have some fun. Before my job, I thought life was a painful struggle that had no rewards." Work can mean life to an older person who finds work a tool to bridge the gap between deprivation and the ability to satisfy basic needs.

If I am a workaholic, I pay a price. The compulsion to be busy and task-oriented excludes or impedes many experiences. To recreate, to wonder, to do nothing are practically absent. As we have seen, love can be taken for granted and at best precariously maintained instead of continually promoted. In time, I become increasingly aware that much of life has passed and is passing by.

If not before, I am likely to experience a crisis upon retirement. I may feel that I am being put out to pasture to lead a useless life—that retiring from work means retiring from life. Although I may be very efficient and successful, I may feel frightened when there is less energy and reason to work and may feel confused when I find myself working at working. Fighting myself, I become more tired and older than I ought to be—and, coming closer to death, I may die, at least spiritually, before my time.

Think of this retirement syndrome. I may try to extend my work beyond sixty-five. Eventually I retire, or thinking I will really enjoy life, I may retire sooner. If wealthy, I may busy myself with travel and activities and may delude myself for several years, but boredom and emptiness finally catch me. I get tired of running and perhaps of living, and I become depressed and scared. My work approach makes little sense when life beckons me to play, wonder, surrender, celebrate, love. Or I may search intensely for work, and after fixing everything twice. I get uptight and feel that I am in the way. Then I may try hobbies or social activities, but they too become meaningless. Eventually, I can become bored to death. Being with myself in time, I can feel anxiously helpless when I hear the voice of death say: "Live!"

Sometimes part-time jobs can help bridge the gap between work and non-work lives. Such a part-time job, however, should not be a way to run from life, but a means of structuring time for productive and enjoyable experiences. Consider this man's retirement work. Owning an old house, he often finds something to clean, fix, or paint, and he helps his son, at least weekly, with cutting the grass and various projects inside and outside the house. They always seem to be building, planning, or planting something together so that they maintain and produce, and more importantly, enjoy each other. During the winter, this 72-year-old man works with and enjoys his wife's company, visits his children, and reads considerably. He feels more alive and fulfilled than ever before.

We should prepare for retirement—for activities we always wanted to do and for enjoying everyday living with ourselves and others. The crucial preparation is to live an integral life before retirement. If we have led fragmented lives in being workaholics, we can hardly expect to be happy upon retirement. Actually, when retired, we should have the wisdom to enjoy life more than ever, and if we live whole lives before retirement, retirement can be the culmination of life.

Workism is not only a masculine mode of madness, for any mode of madness can involve both females and males. Workism, however, may have lent itself more to men mainly because more men than women have traditionally been the "workers." Furthermore, men are programmed to gain their self-esteem from work achievement, while women are more likely to learn to acquire self-esteem from interpersonal relationships. But the roles of women are changing, and career workism may also snare more women. Then everyone and everything are in service of her work so that when she retires from work, she also retires from life. Although she may lead a well-adjusted and "successful" life, her life may lack personal and interpersonal fulfillment. Her sublimation of love leads to sublimation of life.

Or consider religious who profess that their life is a life of service. Too often such religious (and clerics) identify service with work so that they have extreme difficulty in "doing nothing." They may find themselves too tired to pray, too preoccupied to meditate, too tense to play, too busy to relax. Or reading a novel may evoke comments like "I wish that I had time to read," or "Don't you have anything better to do?", and soon the religious feels guilty for "wasting time." When not working or when retired, some religious feel guilty, worthless, depressed, or lost. And others may feel angry and resentful for being pressured to be workaholics. Thus, those people who vow to give witness to spiritual values may also become disciples of workism. Though they may call their madness service, work is too often primary while spirituality is secondary.

Or I may be a housewife who probably works more than most other workers, is seldom paid, and is often taken for granted. I can become so involved with the house, children, and perhaps extra-familial activities that loving interplay with my husband and children is lost. For instance, I can be thrown into a crisis when my husband retires. Suddenly, I wonder what I am going to do with him. I might say: "I don't know what to do with him. He always gets in the way. I wish he did something. He's always moping around the house." I may also find that I am getting older, have less time, and work makes less sense to me especially if I am a workaholic. My children are gone, and perhaps few if any grandchildren visit often. Coming from a life of compulsive activity, I may find myself having relatively nothing to do. Death also summons me to live. If my style has been to work at life, I may feel helpless in responding to the voice of death.

If I and my husband learned only to live a normal life—to adjust to and to be content with each other, we will look at each other as strangers. But if we have grown closer together, this can be our best time. We have truly become two in one, and know and sense each other inside and out. We enjoy growing older together.

What if I discover that I am a workaholic, or like many of us, have tendencies toward workism. I must first admit that I am or can be a workaholic, and then I can combat and use creatively my propensities toward workism. I can take stock of myself and honestly review what values are most important—not just in theory but in everyday living. I may sincerely say that my personal vocation is more important than work, but if I am too preoccupied to be wholly present to my community, too busy to play, or too tired to love, then I am fooling myself. What happens in experience, not theory, is what counts.

Because of my madness, I can restructure my life to promote fuller living. I can use my vice to promote virtue. For example, I can take time for solitude not when it is convenient but consistently and perhaps daily. In solitude I can slow down, listen to, and reflect on life. I can structure parts of my life for play— not simply when I have time but to set times just as firmly as I do for work. For example, buying season tickets for aesthetic and cultural events may pressure me to be leisurely with my spouse or friend. And if I cannot afford such events, I can enjoy free and natural events and I can consistently take time for family or friends instead of working overtime or hiding behind a newspaper. Whatever I do, I must set structures that allow me to be with, converse, recreate, reflect, and to promote other activities that are at least as important as work. Knowing that I can be a workaholic can actually motivate me to transcend my madness.

Unfortunately, my madness is not only in my hands. To go beyond normal madness means that I must go beyond my culture. We have seen that our culture promotes normal madness especially one like workism. I must be careful not to be seduced by the cultural applause that affirms and promotes workism and be willing to accept and cope with the cultural flack that may come from not being a workaholic. Thinking that making love is more important than making money is seldom culturally reinforced and rewarded.

I may also have to make sacrifices. If I can make much more money or climb the success ladder at the expense of community happiness, what do I do? Do I keep a meaningful and liberating job that has less social recognition rather than work where I am forced to play games? Is my personal presence more important than my financial presents? Can I limit my service so I can increase solitude, leisure, and love? What is the measure of my worth? Production? Service? (If so, people like retirees, handicapped, physically and mentally ill, mentally retarded, children, and preborn are in jeopardy). Experientially, is love paramount? Is everything secondary to and in service of love?

POWERISM

Powerism essentially incorporates functional power as the central motivating force in one's life. If I am a power person, my style is likely to be a clear thinker, to control emotions, and to manipulate everything and everyone. I try to be on top of everything and want nothing to be on top of me. From this position, I can organize and handle anything and anybody efficiently.

Since everything is a means to an end, experiences in themselves are minimized. For example, sex may be used to procreate children, to reduce tension, or to pacify another. In love I must be in control and probably know about the latest psychological techniques, but to be mindless, to let go, to move with the rhythm of love is rare. Everything and everybody revolves around and is in service of my satisfaction and success. And I am likely to hide my true feelings from myself and others behind a facade of functional power which I acquire from my roles. Failing to be the author of my life, I abuse functional authority and become authoritarian.

I am mad because I think I know what is best for everyone. I tell people what to do, and if they refuse my orders, I dismiss, ignore, or withdraw from them. Or being more sophisticated, I make them feel guilty if they resist my "suggestions." Seeing others in terms of competition and manipulation, my goals are victory and subjugation. Giving is infested with conditions that emerge from and reinforce my will to power, and the need to control precludes letting go and being with another. To receive another unconditionally makes little sense.

Powerism can lend itself to and promote workism. At work, I can more easily boss or use people to achieve my ends—and, I may be financially rewarded for my manipulation. Especially if I have a powerful position, I can control more than in personal situations. Family and friends are more likely to rebel against my power tactics and they may be freer to withdraw from me. Most work usually calls for or tolerates task-oriented, manipulative behavior; whereas, more personal and less functional situations tolerate or reject such behavior. Of course, some parents and superiors manage to be power mad with people in their own family and community.

Like any normal mode of madness, powerism makes sense. My (or a nation's) mastery over things and people can give me an illusion of security. I think that I know exactly where I stand and that I can control other people's stands. My willfulness can give me a sense of solidarity and strength, and people may initially admire me because I may witness to many values they prize. It may seem that I am always in control of situations, can make things work, achieve goals, and be successful.

Part of the nonsense is that my will power is often a reaction against underlying feelings of helplessness and inadequacy. Perhaps I learned to be always in control and was punished when I was out of control or acted spontaneously. Or interpersonal intimacy may have been minimized or experienced as sources of rejection. In any case, I overcompensate for hidden weakness in facing personal experiences. Mysterious and paradoxical experiences, lacking certainty and clarity, are threatening and are rationalized as sophomoric. I do not realize that I am the biggest fool. My style becomes a constant compensation for repressed feelings of inadequacy in personal and transcendent realms. To listen openly is too threatening, to reflect thoughtfully is upsetting, to give myself unconditionally is frightening.

My existence is a tragic self-deception. I eventually become aware of my basic helplessness, of the weakness of my power. For instance, because of my compulsion to talk about myself and inability to listen to and appreciate others, people eventually withdraw from me. Besides being alienated, life progressively fragments and efficiency slowly dissipates. While young, I can usually maintain myself and be skillful in normal living. In my personal life I question the meaning of life, and really wonder what all my power and efficiency have meant. Although I have become compulsive and skilled in the art of control, I sense that as I grow older I will have less to control.

I find myself in a new bind: The main approach I know—control and manipulation—do not work. In fact, life becomes worse. I may become lonely, bored, and disgusted and in a panic, try to control more than ever or try to escape in activities like drinking. Perhaps in a desperate and mad attempt to experience spiritual fulfillment, I have a sexual affair. But instead of becoming powerful and stronger, I eventually become powerless and weaker. Everyone and everything I control loses its meaning and no longer gives me secure satisfaction. I begin to realize the temporary quality of my super normality—that permanent meaning is present in its absence. I find myself crying out for what I have forgotten—spirituality.

Ultimately, I am caught in the quagmire of a meaningless and groundless existence. I lose control of life and life overpowers me. I become broken and lost. My willful life has left me will-less. I may eventually find myself in a stagnant depression that says: "You have lost life." Theoretically, I can gain insight and change my life by myself; concretely, it is very difficult. Usually I need a consoling professional or nonprofessional person to help me find the courage and way to change.

To become fully alive, I must experience liberating pain. Through a painful awareness, I can own up to what I am instead of becoming what I am not. I can understand and learn from my history—that I was probably helped and hindered. I can review my life and admit how I and society have repressed my full potential. It is possible to renew myself by discovering and realizing a fuller life. Often in an interpersonal situation, I can experience the meaning of life not primarily as a mater of controlling and being on top of life but basically as a matter of respecting and promoting life. I can see that the joy of living includes mystery that engenders new strength to let go.

I can also be careful of my demonic powers and re-channel my will to power into a willingness to promote fuller living. By claiming my willfullness, maybe I can liberate myself. I can honestly acknowledge how I manipulate others and really see if I have alternate ways of behaving. For instance, I can make a conscious effort to encourage others to talk and to listen to them with interest. I may surprise myself in that I can be available to others in that I can risk sharing myself and letting others touch me. Trying to understand what another feels and letting others get close to me may engender new possibilities. Putting myself in situations like play, solitude, and love can also help me to experience the power of respect and surrender.

I can come to realize where permanent power resides. Instead of rational functionality, transrational spirituality becomes my paramount way to an inexhaustible source of power. Instead of depending on what I have—knowledge, skill, money, things, my power is a matter of who and what I am. Love is the force that keeps me progressively alive. Living in love incorporates and evokes a powerful spirit.

THINKISM

The one who lives according to thinkism is the ultimate rational animal. Hyper-rationality, clear and distinct ideas, and theoretical approaches are symptomatic of this style. The main assumptions are that thinking is the best way to make sense of any experience and that rationality is the ultimate source of truth.

If I am a thinkaholic, I always try to see life as a series of problems that can be analyzed and solved so that nothing is beyond rational explanation. I live and am out of my mind. My main values come from the neck up and anything from the neck down is minimized, repressed, or rationalized. Common sense is inferior sense, and feelings are minimized, repressed, or rationalized. An indifferent detachment toward any emotional involvement is likely so that I present myself as if I were a disembodied mind.

Making rationality my ultimate concern, I live more in theoretical than in experiental worlds. By seeing life in terms of a static and closed framework, I may absolutize a particular theory to the exclusion of other theories and especially of experience. Any situation I am confronted with is interpreted in light of theory, and what does not fit my theory, a person for example, is thrown out. Instead of changing my theory, I throw out the experience. I also am apt to manipulate, distort, or deny any experience that is not congruent with my approach. For example, I usually misunderstand people because they are seen only in light of my theories and explanations. Although I may quickly explain the reason for a person's behavior, I fail to truly understand. Instead of getting into the world of others, I unconsciously and perhaps with concern use them to affirm my own thinking. My onesided approach enables me to operate efficiently, to maintain myself, to adjust and compromise, and to keep safely in control.

Although we may not be strict advocates of thinkism, we can have tendencies toward or be influenced by thinkism especially if we are in "heady atmospheres." It can be tempting to operate according to a particular rational approach. For instance, I may opt for the madness of scientism: I believe that science will eventually explain and account for any phenomenon and that any meaning beyond the world of science is secondary or irrelevant. Meta-scientific experience is an illusion. Since my approach is to be objective, systematic, and rational, I seldom involve myself spontaneously, surrender, or simply have fun. Instead, I become a rigid scientist who takes only an objective, systematic, and rational look at life.

A form of scientism is psychologism. As an advocate of psychologism, I psychologize: I always have a psychological explanation for a person's behavior. Instead of taking the risk of really being involved with people, I can simply analyze and explain them. Because of my psychological know-how, I think I have the right and perhaps the obligation to say what is true for another—to interpret the meaning of people's experience or solve their problems. I assume that I know better than the people themselves—that I am the way, the light, and the truth. Lacking in such psychological arrogance is a genuine respect and appreciation of others, (the humility that affirms that any person or situation is infinitely more than what I think), and the openness and courage to let life emerge. Hiding behind my psychological mask, I can play God and often have my subjects pay and applaud me.

Or I may take a philosophical approach. Everything has deep, complicated and serious meaning, everything involves everything else, and nothing is simple about life. To really know the truth, I must sit for hours and discuss the philosophical implications. I think I can philosophically understand and analyze everything, and the non-rational, trans-rational, and irrational are seen as inferior and invalid. Like most thinkistic people, I am tight, too serious, and lack warmth. I can waste a lot of time and energy planning programs rather than living life. I can think (and perhaps teach) much about living but forget to live.

All these and other approaches of thinkism can give me a false sense of security, enable me to look good, and can engender some convenience in coping with situations. I can delude myself into thinking that any experience can be analyzed and made clear—that every act can be rationally explained. The culture may also support and prize my rationalism. Many people assume that rationality is the highest form of knowledge and is an ideal of maturity. Not to think or to be purely present may be considered nice, but not as important as cognition. To contemplate is a fringe benefit or a means to improve rationality. To teach people to be mindless would be considered absurd.

As long as I hold onto my thoughts, I do not have to surrender and risk myself to the unknown. Like the power person, I am on top of things and know where I stand. Everything is explicit; nothing is implicit. Lacking is a sense of mystery, faith, and surprise. To kid is sophomoric; to celebrate is wasteful; to feel intensely is sentimentalism. The knowledge of feelings and mystery is precariously beyond comprehension. While expanding my mind, I strangle my heart. The more I think about life, the less I am present in an enjoyable and whole way. For instance, if I happen to experience a sunset, I am likely to analyze my experience and the more I analyze it, the less I experience the sunset. Before long, I am occupied with the thought instead of the real thing—with second-hand instead of first-hand knowledge.

Some people may experience me as coldly strong and solidly empty, highly informed but actually shallow. After listening to me, you might hear a programmed person who covers instead of uncovers life. Words may initially seem to make sense, but soon they sound manipulative and boring. My sharp and systematic approach cuts away the flesh of living. Presenting theories and explanations instead of myself, I display a strange sense of inhuman perfection.

Am I condemned to living out of my mind? One of my main tasks is (metaphorically) to cut off my head. Can I discipline myself not to think so I can listen to and see more than my mind comprehends? Can I stop the artificial world of theoretical analysis and experience the world anew? Can I go beyond my categories and be present to different actualities? Can I experience the inexhaustible meaning of a tree, animal, or person rather than passing them by or taking them for granted.

Perhaps I can discover life beyond the rubrics of my mind. I must realize that my thoughts are perspectives on a greater whole and that they are partial—biased parts of experience. I must struggle to let life emerge, to speak, to embrace me instead of manipulating, dictating, and being against life. By claiming my compulsion to think, I can motivate myself to suspend my thoughts in order to listen, wonder about, and see beyond the surface of rational knowledge.

Still this can be scary. When I let go of my clear and distinct ideas, I may be initially left with nothing. I may find myself in a desert where I fast rather than indulge, hear silence rather than applause, see nothing rather than something. But if I accept creatively rather than resist or escape from the limits of my existence, I can experience what underlies and gives life to all my boundaries. I can come to refreshing and revitalizing sense. I can come to see unity even in dissension, to enjoy the mystery of underlying problems, and to dance to the sound of life.

Various approaches and methods that can facilitate this spiritual quest have been promoted throughout history. Spiritual writers from various times are still significant and helpful to our spiritual search. Methods like meditation, spiritual reading, and personal journals may be more prevalent than we may realize. And spiritual movements, houses of prayer, and spiritual literature can also indicate a thrust for meaning beyond the rational. There are many ways; my challenge and call is to find my way. If I am not to be suffocated by my mind, I must continually struggle to breathe as a whole being.

FEELISM

Advocates of feelism feel that relevant truth comes from their guts, not from their heads like thinkaholics. To really feel and to express feelings solve any problems, and sincerity and honesty make everything okay. If I am such a feeling person, I am present-oriented—I only live in and for the "here and now." Although I am apt to criticize tradition and structure, I can be very sensitive. Full expression of feelings becomes, in fantasy or in reality, the "in" thing. Investing my energies in feelings, I may seem vibrantly real and fully alive. People may admire, envy, or be afraid of me, but in whatever case, I am usually recognized. My affective and dynamic style draws attention, demands response, and makes indifference unlikely.

Although I live to have fun and to care, my experiences can too often be forced and contrived. I can become a caricature of what I want to be. For example, I may frequent groups (or form a community) where most of us may glow with care and affection, but actually we play a game of perfect concern instead of really meeting one another. And those "unfortunates" who do not play our game are patronized, pressured to feel guilty, or prayed for so they might reach our level of "maturity." Although we may constantly talk about love and make loving gestures, our love tends to be a pretense that lacks respect, pain, and fidelity.

I may try to live the fantasy that love can be a panacea for everything. Feeling that love will solve all problems and create a utopian life, I fail to realize that love in itself solves little. For example, loving mentally ill people twenty-four hours a day will not help them much, besides being impossible because constant explicit love results in tense exhaustion. Any approach, however, that excludes love fails to heal. My goal is to learn to implement love in the most therapeutic way, and this takes study and work. The fantasy of "love in itself" can be a way of escaping the effort and responsibility of real love.

Sometimes some of us protest the confines of acceptable behavior and form counter culture groups; for instance, we may establish communities to practice open love with encouraged sharing. We may try to be completely open but we soon find that we need solitude, respectful distance, and free closedness. We come to realize that to grow in community means love and life must be implemented with a respect and appreciation for the various rhythms of distance and closeness, of readiness and untimeliness, of "yes" and "no."

Our key words are openness, honesty, sincerity, encounter, confrontation, presence, sharing, love, and feel. Too often, however, our openness masks closedness, honesty hides truth, sincerity is simplistic, presence forces absence, sharing is manipulative, love is conditional, and feelings are impulsive.

To be a truly open person, I must try to admit my limits, imperfections, biases—ways I am not, cannot, or will not be open. Part of growing in openness is to affirm, learn from, and cope with closedness toward self and others. Pure openness is a myth. To be healthy, I have to admit that honesty and sincerity are ways to truth rather than guarantees of or the same as truth. To transcend feelism, I admit that I am capable of honestly and sincerely satisfying myself at the expense of others, of using others as means for self-gratification. I realize that in the name of openness I can rip off masks and psychologically rape people, that intrusive presence evokes protective withdrawal instead of secure closeness. I come to know how easy it is to love people who agree with me, cause me no pain, and like me. Out of love, I strive to temper and creatively control feelings. Although I try to be aware of all my feelings, I express feelings that help instead of hinder.

I know that feelings are an important source of truth, that though they are ambivalent and preconscious, feelings seldom lie. Also realized is that thought and inspiration are as important and can be more important than feelings. I am aware of the madness in absolutizing the truth of feelings and in exploiting others to achieve catharsis—that though my madness can give satisfaction, pleasure, and affective power, I rob myself and others of creative discipline, responsible love, and spiritual strength.

GENITALISM

In the madness of genitalism, my ultimate concern is genital sex. Genital sexuality refers to behavior that directly involves or promotes genital gratification. Being sexualistic means that I see sex as the guiding force in life. Though I may deny that I live according to a sex principle that posits sex as my primary value, experientially my life betrays me. My style and presence to others are colored by and geared toward genital achievement. In experiencing others ultimately as objects to be used for sexual satisfaction, I see and make people less than they are. My world—the ways I experience reality—become genitalized so that almost every body and thing are possibilities for genital gratification.

Although I can be sophisticated and show concern for others, my behavior is basically in service of self-satisfaction. So when I do not get what I want, I withdraw and look for somebody else. I am a normal madman because I live according to a playboy philosophy: I am not a mature person, but a boy who plays. Being immersed in this, I can appear vital and carefree, but I fail to grow in depth and permanency.

Some people may admire me as a playboy. It seems that I am really enjoying life and constantly having new experiences, and people who emphasize maintenance may admire my dynamism. And I may have the looks and techniques to get what I want. Although I may have a high aptitude for violence, I may seldom be overtly intrusive and disruptive. My violence is subtle, and consequently I am at least accepted as normal.

The ease and availability of sex encourage and facilitate my sexualism. It is easier than in the past for sexualistic people to find partners and to move in public without embarrassment. Social establishments like bars, clubs, and apartments may cater to my seeking sex. Prostitution and pornography also feed and stimulate my hunger. Without much difficulty they supply my demands and help to maintain and promote my madness. The prostitute diagnoses and treats my madness, and her fee varies according to her expertise and treatment. Pornography stimulates my genitalism by taking sex out of a healthy context. The easy excitement and immediate gratification may seem more attractive than enthusiastic wholeness.

Genitalism makes sense. Genital activity can satisfy basic needs, take away tension, and help me feel at peace. If I feel basically at odds with myself, I can feel a certain completeness and tranquility along with quasi-fun. If I am a workaholic, genital sex can offer an easy relief from the business of everyday life.

If I am a thinkaholic, sexualism can be especially seductive. At least for awhile, I do not have to think about living, but I can more or less let myself go. Sex may serve to numb my perpetual mentation and offer my mind needed rest. Or if I am lonely, sexual involvement may seem like good sense. Even though I may realize I am being exploited, I may feel worthy enough to be used. Sometimes anything seems better than nothing—and besides, sexuality is a normal and easy affirmation of life. Most people do not celebrate celibacy.

The power of sexuality can become narcissistic and mad. For instance, I can feel power in my ability "to make" and penetrate a woman. Or I can feel powerful in making the male helpless in my arms while smiling at his impotent chauvenism. Whether a sexual madman or madwoman, I use the other and degrade myself.

A clue to genital madness may be that a desire for power is a compensation for inferiority toward one's own and the other sex. Perhaps more men than women use genital power as a means of compensating for inadequate identity and fear of sex. In sexual exploits men can feel powerful in exploiting women. Such genital encounters are used to make up for a tenuous sense of identity.

Being sexualistic, I am mad because my sex is without care, responsibility, and commitment. When I exploit others and see them as less than they are, I violate both them and myself. My behavior does not promote emergent and integral living, but basically maintains and can destroy life. My madness prevents me from hearing the deeper call of genital sex—love. Being concrete and creative, sex calls for responsibility and commitment. Since sex without love only gives temporary satisfaction—not permanent fulfillment, genitalism ultimately leads to frustration and emptiness.

In time, my sexual spirit cries out. Besides having less energy, attraction, and desire, I hear the call of other realities. Loveless sex is no longer as vital and exciting as it once was, and it fails to answer my deeper questions. Sex fails to meet the summons of impending death—to live fully and wholly. In facing death, I find that I am dissociated and displaced—cut off from my spirit. My sexual search for meaning eventually leaves me lifeless.

In separating sex and love, I use myself and others as sex objects. I actually lack respect for myself because I treat myself as less than I am. I violate myself when I see my main meaning coming from sex—and, I violate sex by demanding that sex do what only love can—make me a whole person. My care-less sex leaves me without care, and my vitality leads to death. I become a broken and spiritless person.

My hope rests in listening to the neglected aspects of myself. I can look behind my facade of nudity and respond to my yearning for integrity. But to love is much more risky than playing sexual games. Perhaps I can understand that my sexual madness is a search for permanent meaning—that in my madness is my hope. Although I can hide more easily in genital sex than in the openness of love, I must touch and care for my whole self if I am to be more than part of myself. I must integrate sexuality and spirituality to be wholly me.

Similar to and differing from conventional genitalism is homogenitalism—having genital sex with the same sex as my highest value. I am a homogenital when my central motivating force is to have homogenital relations. Both heterogenitalism and homogenitalism are modes of normal madness, though heterogenitalism is much more accepted, promoted, and reinforced. Social sanctions tend to be for heterogenitalism and against homogenitalism.

When homosexuality is equated with homogenitality, misleading assumptions can occur because men should show affection to men and women to women. That is, a person is healthy when he or she actualizes his or her sexual-spiritual self, though not genitally, with the same sex. This distinction can be important because many people, especially men, have much difficulty being intimate or affectionate with the same sex.

Many professionals and non-professionals have ambivalent feelings about homogenitality. Some feel that homogenitality is an illness or a symptom of illness; others think it is a sign of perversion or a sign of "unmanliness," and still others consider it a different sexual orientation that can be healthy or unhealthy. Our approach is that homosexuality or homosociality—love between persons of the same sex—is necessary and healthy, and homogenitality—genital relations between members of the same sex—is normally mad though not meaningless.

Homogenitalism is genitalism with the same sex. If I am homogenital, I exclude intimacy with the other sex and make genitality with the same sex my ultimate source of fulfillment. I, too, am an advocate of genitalism, and though I am similar to my mad and "straight" heterogenital brother, I also differ. My basic lifestyle is homogenital because I only feel comfortable in intimacy with the same sex. When I am too close to a woman (or she with a man), I feel uncomfortable, angry, or simply turned off, but with men, I feel at home. I feel affirmed and fulfilled. And when I feel fragmented, lonely, or empty, I often seek genital relations in a mad attempt to make everything all right. Homogenital sex is my way to satisfaction and contentment.

Like a heterogenital, I lack lasting commitment in my cruising search for wholeness. Although I can be authentic in my struggle for love, my genital compulsion ends in futility because my genital relationships do not bring progressive and lasting commitment. Although they differ secondarily, both homogenitalism and heterogenitalism are normal and mad modes of sexual existence.

Still, I may grow in permanence and completion in friendship that is affectionate though not genital. And my work can also be an avenue of integrity and lasting meaning. Instead of totalizing and centering my life around homogenitality, I can strive to be a person who loves all of life. Like my mad heterogenital brother, I, too, can struggle for wholeness. I can strive to love, show affection, to both men and women.

RELIGIONISM

I can be a person who knows all the religious rules, attends the right activities, is a pillar of the church, and yet not live a truly religious life. Although I know about religion, I am not religious. I am the religious hypocrite whom the community and church too often support and praise, for I am usually a temperate person who does all the right things when watched.

Although I may even be admired,, I am often mad. I live too much according to standards and rules, not according to life. I support structures instead of people, and I talk better than I live. For example, I may get involved in various social activities and do charitable works while I give little love to my family and community. Or instead of showing love, I preach and teach love while acting hostilely and breeding resentment. My ministry hinders more than helps—confuses more than unifies. I can put up a fruitful front that hides a decaying process.

My madness may mean that I not only know what is right for myself but also know what is right for others. Unfortunately, my moral arrogance is often accepted by others. People may even help me to deceive myself by expecting that I know all the answers for everyone. In looking to me for the source of the truth instead of within themselves, they reinforce my self-deception. Others, however, may resent me—a person who knows the right words, looks down on people, and hides behind a sermon of love rather than facing people with love.

I am mad because I play the game of being God and because I am actually estranged from what I stand for—deeper spiritual experiences. Transcendence, compassion, and love are missing. Following the structure of religious experience—religion, instead of promoting a religious life, I become a caricature of what I want to be. Although I may look good, inside I lack genuine love —the essence of religion.

One of my projects is to experience what I preach—religious experience. For example, I can promote prayer, reflective reading, and meditation, and strive to experience meaning in liturgical services. To follow and learn from a spiritual mentor can be especially beneficial. And again, I must be willing to suffer my dark nights to receive the gift of enlightment.

Paramount is to live a life of love. Although it is safer and easier to hide behind religionism instead of exposing and giving myself in love, nothing much happens except alienation and emptiness in myself and hurt and resentment in others. I must learn to implement my love in service of others.

CLASSISM

Some people's mode of madness centers around maintaining an "upper class" level of living. In this madness, certain standards of behavior are set; and only behavior fitting these standards is accepted. Certain behavior is proper or improper—"proper" being the key word. The proper thing is the thing to have, do, and be—and one in a certain class can, should, and must be proper. Proper is what the majority of a class thinks is necessary to maintain superiority.

Consider a phoney proper dinner. Speech is repetitive and calculated; understanding is brief and shallow; feelings are restricted and hidden; dress is expensive and protective; posture is straight and proud; movement is quiet and static; drinking is subtle and eating is satisfying. Animation, earthiness, listening, bending, depth, color, emotion, motion, and feasting are absent. The evening is quite proper.

Proper behavior is expected, sanctioned, and rewarded; while improper behavior is unexpected, embarrassing, and punished. When a proper person does something improper, we proper people are surprised and embarrassed and try to change and cover the behavior as quickly as possible. For example, if I as a member of a proper family speak improperly, I am ignored, minimized, or rationalized. And if I refuse to play the game, I am explicitly or implicitly ostracized.

Being proper usually deals with my external behavior and

seldom has much to do with my inner experience. I can feel almost anything as long as I behave properly with others. I can learn to be an expert in covering reality. I can build powerful facades to hide my backstage activities (where improper behavior may occur), and I often enter into collusion with others to maintain the illusion of propriety.

Proper activities protect me by letting me speak only within my framework. For example, I may repeat stock phrases to sound intelligent, but when challenged to pursue a subject, I change the subject or withdraw from the situation. I put up the front of being bright, but in fact I may be shallow and dull. To speak in depth of ideals, personal values, or death is not very proper, and consequently need not be talked about. In being proper, I can easily project pleasant fronts that hide painful realities. Occasionally, perhaps under the influence of alcohol, I will take off my mask and show my true colors, and I may use language that is highly improper and say what is seldom said. Soon, however, I return to my proper self and pretend that everything is all right. Things are back to normal.

We proper people can play covert games—"Who Has the Most," "Who Has the Most Prestigious Job," "Who Does the Most," "Who Has the Best Vocabulary, Most Information, and Best Wardrobe," "Who Gives the Most and Best," "Who Belongs to the Most and the Best," "Who Has the Most Friends," "Who is the Most Proper!" Some of the contradictory rules are: be independent, be like everyone else, have friends, do not be intrusive, know what is going on, be proper. Above all, stay in proper formation! Do not be abnormal—for example, have too different a house, speak and look differently, or be more than content. The winner of the game is envied, admired, and hated. The unhappy losers strive to win—and envy, admire, and hate. The abnormal person who is not in proper formation is seen as eccentric or mad, certainly not proper, and is tolerated, ostracized, or dismissed as a person with no "class."

If we are people of classism, we can try to make or keep others (those not in our class) sufficiently "lower" to give ourselves the illusion of status and power. For example, race A may see race B as "potentially" equal, making race A superior. Certain ethnic groups may be seen as intelligently inferior, making other ethnic groups superior. One sex may patronize the other by "giving them opportunities as long as they stay in their place" and thus insure their sexual superiority. So-called straight men may need homosexuals to strengthen their (straight) precarious sexual identity. So-called higher (especially economic) classes can look down on and perhaps displace frustration and anger on so-called lower classes or perhaps pity and manipulate them in the name of philanthropy. Pulling rank can give us the illusion of being better, higher, and stronger.

My "class" may mean that I pull rank on people with "no class." Regardless of the other's worth, I assume that the other is inferior. I may cheerfully tolerate or sincerely patronize the lower class person, but I never seriously consider that the other may be worth as much as or more than I. The other's contribution is never seriously respected and listened to. The assumption is that a lower class person could never be equal to or above me—a higher class person.

Part of my madness is that I often have the power to pull unjust rank and make other people feel guilty for not playing my game or for being inferior to me. Strongly assuming my superiority, I can make others feel lower or withdraw in confusion. I often intimidate people who may appear to be crude but who may actually be better and more educated. Many people, furthermore, support my madness in assuming that the trained and pseudo-sophisticated person is better than the person with "no class."

Rank-pulling can give me the illusion of superiority and power. As long as I can convince myself and others that some people are lower, I can feel higher. No matter who the lower persons are or what they do, I look down on them. Out of frustration, anger, and resentment, the lowered persons may try to pull me down to equal status. Or they may acquiesce and act as if they are worthless. Or they may see through my masks and manifest their dignity.

Most significantly, I try to deceive myself and others with behavioral masks that hide or filter the pure presence of love. My love becomes oblique, distant, and perhaps forgotten. I slowly become alienated from myself and others, including those who are close to me—like family and friends. To be truly present to and for others, I must first be open to myself. I must accept in love my own possible self-centeredness, my propensity to manipulate, and my fear of giving and receiving in love. I can begin to reach out and touch in love. Though such an appeal is risky, life is at stake.

I can also strive to listen to others which includes being quiet and hearing what others are really saying. Instead of minimizing their value, I appreciate and learn from them. To accept (not necessarily to condone, agree, or disagree with) what a person is trying to express, and above all to love (not necessarily like) unconditionally. My goal is to see the ground common to all of us regardless of class, and then to celebrate our being together. Living in the spirit of love, we are one.

PARENTISM

Parentism occurs when being a parent is my main function, ultimate value, and fundamental source of meaning. The madness can center around the unconscious use of children to satisfy my own needs. I may love children because I have no one else to love, or I may manipulate their lives to achieve my own goals. I may even try to produce a great number of children because it gives me a false sense of identity and posterity.

Similar to classism, I may gain meaning and comfort from pulling rank. I only feel competent and content in reference to someone who is younger and supposedly more ignorant than I. I feel I can really be myself when I can judge and tell people (children) what to do, but in other situations, I may feel uncomfortable and inadequate. For instance, children can easily serve as scapegoats for my frustrated feelings. I can displace my anger and hostility on children who become helpless victims of my immaturity. Children cannot do much except get angry, pout, or withdraw, and then they are labeled immature or obstinate and punished. I refuse to realize that children's behavior can be a realistic response to my immaturity. Although anyone can succumb to such madness, parents and teachers are prime candidates.

A child, who is dependent, really cannot protest very much if my concern is too conditional. If I convey to the child, "If you do this, then I will love you," the child's experience of being loved is too contingent upon behavior. Or if I constantly tell the child "no" without any kind of "yes," understanding, or discussion, the child can live in a world of "nos" that can too easily stifle growth. Certainly, within the context of love, limits and restrictions are not only possible but necessary; however, these directives should be in service of unconditional love, not vice versa. A challenge is to promote the free and disciplined spirit of children, not stifle or kill their spirit.

A popular form of parentism is motherism. Motherism occurs when being a mother permeates and guides my entire life so that I identify totally with being a mother and fail to realize myself in other ways. I eat, sleep, breathe for my children so that other interests or activities, including being a whole person, do not exist for me. Fatherism is not a dominant mode of madness partly because many fathers spend too little time with their children and because of sexist prejudice. The few men who do make fatherhood their ultimate concern often become milquetoasts who feel compelled to cater to their children and wife.

Though the mad development of a child is often blamed more on a mother, a father can be just as mad as or madder than a mother. For instance, a young person may not see father very much. If dad is not working, he is often with "the boys"—golf, cards, drinking—playing with anyone except his wife and children. In particular, workaholic men may not take the interest, time and energy to be good fathers, and playboy fathers would rather play than be with their family. These and other masculine failures increase the odds for motherism and lost children. The woman is overburdened and frequently becomes resentful and overprotective, and the children may learn to lack a sense of solidarity, initiative, and identity. When these lost children become adults, they feel cheated and "scream" for their identity. Or even though as young adults they may have protested against their parents, they may later repeat their parent's mad behavior when they themselves become parents.

The fact is that many women are forced to take too much responsibility in raising children. They are expected to be inexhaustible sources of patience, understanding, and acceptance—and, they often feel guilty when they do not meet these unrealistic goals. Many mothers are expected and expect of themselves never to be angry, irritable, envious, or bored. This mystique of motherhood promotes depressed and guilty women—spiritless women.

Momism differs from but can be related to motherism. Momism means that little boys and girls grow up to be big boys and girls, and it occurs when smothering mothers and phantom fathers reinforce dependency. Followers of momism are hyperdependent on their mothers, and they feel good only when their mothers psychologically bless them. Thus, when mothers promote momism, they also insure their own madness in motherism. They increase the probability that their children will be dependent on them for the rest of their lives.

If I am caught in motherism, a crisis often occurs in my thirties. Since my children are probably in school, I may find myself with more free time to re-evaluate my life and to consider other interests. I may feel much older than I really am and yet feel that I am ignorant to worlds other then my world of motherhood. The time may be ripe to be bored, to engage in outside activities, to have an affair, or to deepen my life.

When motherhood ends—the children leave, my life may end.

Since most of my spirit was invested in my children, I may have no other activities, do not know my husband, and become depressed. I am no longer an active mother, do not know the meaning of being a wife, and sell myself short as a person. Such a mother can pay the price of alienation, boredom, and depression—feelings that call for more integral living.

If I am a depressed father, I may identify my life with my work so that actually I am seldom an authentic father and husband. Working so much and being uptight, I tend to lack warmth and spontaneity with my children and wife. Life also catches up to me. I become a depressed father who never learned to enjoy and to grow deeper in love with my wife and children. I am normal and mad.

To be sure: It is quite possible and all too frequent to go to the opposite extreme of parentism and fail to realize that parenthood is one of the most important and responsible functions and values in life. For instance, if I consider my children as things I own or as less important than other activities, perhaps I should not be a parent. Or to indulge children with things because it is easier than to teach them the discipline necessary for freedom promotes madness. To help children transcend cultural madness and prevent personal madness takes much consistent interest, time, and energy. And if I do not constantly try to improve my parenting, I am being irresponsible. Still, identifying my life with parenthood is almost as mad as being an incompetent and unjust parent.

To get out of the vortex of parentism I must go deeper into it. I must honestly access what I am doing and why. I must also discern what kind of a model I am for my children because if I cheat myself, I cheat my children. Fostering new worlds of meaning in or out of the home or both can help me be a better person and parent.

It may be initially very difficult to change especially if I have little or no support, but it may not be as difficult as I assume. My project is to expand and deepen my life—to be more than a parent. Am I a good husband or wife? Am I a companion? How and how often do I nourish my personal growth? How and how often do I enjoy life outside of parenting? Does life make sense without my children? Am I living a life of love? Am I happy? Can I say "yes," to life?

Remember: We never stop failing completely. Our challenge is to struggle to improve—not to get stuck in a rut and let a lot of life go by. We must be vigilant because we can always be caught in the throes of madness and lose our spirit. Still, we can strive to learn from our madness to be less mad and more healthy—to be more wholly alive.

CHAPTER FOUR

Transactional Madness

"Everyone seems to be playing a role. I see masks, but don't encounter people. It really gets horrible at parties; the phony games are depressing. It appears as though everyone is trying to outdo or impress everyone else. The professionals have their style— and the doctors' wives are something else. And they expect me to play a role too. Just because I'm twenty-two, blonde, and attractive, they're almost shocked when I say something intelligent or when I try to cut through their facades. Once in a while, I'll meet a person who speaks straight. What relief! Why do people have to hide, be phony, and perform? I know it sounds trite, but why can't they just be themselves?

"I should talk; my husband and I can't even share. We try but we just don't make it very often. When I try to say what I really feel, he tries to listen but he rarely understands. Or worse yet, he won't share with me. When he's angry, he gets more angry when I ask him what's going on? Or when I ask him about the way he acts with his professional friends, he says that it's necessary to play roles if you want to get ahead. Does he have to hide from me too? I don't know, it seems that we waste a lot of time hiding from each other."

This woman describes a common and mad experience. We can play games to get ahead and expect others to do the same, and we can hide from one another and pretend we are authentically meeting. And even when we try to share, our efforts to live in community can end in frustration rather than in fulfillment. Instead of facing one another honestly and truthfully, we speak through masks. What should and could be a dialogue becomes a series of monologues. Community dissipates into a collectivity.

Although most of the following transactions are accepted, often approved, and encouraged, they are mad. Instead of being an honest, truthful, and respectful sharing, communication can be consciously or unconsciously dishonest, cover the truth, and be manipulative. Such interpersonal transactions promote alienation rather than unity. Interpersonal madness occurs when we help one another to become estranged from ourselves and from one another. This is not to imply that all relationships should be intimate but that too many are oblique and destructive. Instead of becoming close to one another, we become more distant. Instead of promoting and growing in love, we impede and fall out of love.

PRETENSE

Our mad interpersonal relationships are often based on pretense—a cover that hides unacceptable truth. When pretending, we act as if certain realities do not exist because admitting the forbidden reality would cause unacceptable pain. A show is put on, for ourselves and others, to mask underlying activity. Pretense is a curtain that usually covers and protects us from threatening experiences. Instead of showing and sharing ourselves, we hold something before us—something that clouds and filters our experience. What we feel, think, and believe is not openly communicated— neither to others, nor to ourselves, and consequently we behave and are experienced as less than we really are.

We can pretend, usually unconsciously, for many reasons. For example, a man who feels inferior toward women may pretend to be stronger than women. Always ready to order, pull rank, protect, or insult women, he puts up a strong front that hides underlying weakness. Or a woman who is anxiously uncertain may pretend to be in control of everything. Her smooth show may evoke applause unless her backstage activity is seen.

For instance, such persons may be highly successful and power-ful in career and social affairs, but within their personal com-munity they are seen as hypocritical and weak and are not respected. Consequently, such people may withdraw from their personal commitment and involve themselves totally in social and professional activities.

One lethal game is to pretend to be who you really are. For example, an intelligent woman may be taught to see and treat herself as stupid and inferior, and overcompensating for her poor self-image, she acts as if she were what she really is—intelligent. Within herself, she seldom believes that she really is intelligent, and to make matters worse, people may pretend that she is not pretending. They pretend that she is bright while unconsciously everyone feels that she is not bright. No one admits that she really is intelligent. Thus, people (including herself) seldom value her views as much as others' views, and consequently they minimize her true value and perhaps maximize their own.

Transactions can be based on collusion—two or more persons pretending while pretending that no pretense exists. Collusion is based on mutual self-deception. I say to you: "I'll pretend that you're not pretending, if you pretend that I'm not pretending. And we'll both pretend that we're not pretending." Both of us pretend that we are doing something that we are not, and we add to our madness by pretending that we are not pretending. Life becomes a chaos of collusions. To pretend can be mad or healthy, but to pretend that we are not pretending is mad.

In collusion we meet one another's false projections of our real selves. We pretend to others and to ourselves that non-truth is truth and truth is non-truth. We can even lose the ability and desire to know the difference between the caricature and the real thing. For instance, normal communities can be based on collusion. In marital collusion, we may say to each other: "I'll pretend that our marriage is what it ought to be, and if you pre-tend that I'm not pretending, I'll pretend that your marriage is healthy." We can pretend that our lives are happy and healthy, though they are really boring and mad. It often seems that when we make a personal commitment such as to marriage or religious life, we move out of love instead of deeper into love. We can learn to have a normal community—to adjust to each other, to have a smooth relationship without much tension but without much growth either. Or we can learn to be content with each other—to put up with each other. Too frequently, our communal contract implicitly includes: "If you do not bother me, I will not bother you." Furthermore, most of our friends and neighbors may pretend that their bland lives have enthusiasm. Pretending to one another that we are not pretending, we deceive ourselves and one another. Rather than journeying with one another in love, we adjust or endure one another's lonely and isolated trips.

Strategies based on pretense are ways of hiding or modifying the truth in order to protect ourselves. I pretend, to myself and to others, that I am right where in fact I am wrong. I act as if fallacies were facts and non-truths. For instance, pretending to be honest, I can "project" my feelings of anger onto another person, and the other person can pretend that I am being true. Consider parents who instead of admitting anger to children blame them for feeling angry. Initially, the children are bewildered because they really do not feel angry, but to be accepted and to prevent punishment, they can learn to believe they are angry when they are not, or they can learn to be angry to fulfill the parents' expectations. Their false belief and behavior reinforce the parent's "projective" behavior as well as their own self-deception. And as adults we can re-play such childhood tapes especially in response to authoritarian people, and then feel confused with our behavior.

Or feelings that were originally evoked in one situation may be expressed in another situation. For example, a woman who cannot express anger toward her husband may "displace" her anger on her children. Instead of admitting anger toward her husband, she gets verbally and physically abusive toward an innocent child. Likewise, a person with authority who represses anger toward a higher authority may "dump on" people with less authority—a manager on workers, a coordinator on community members. In a similar fashion, a man bearing unacceptable resentment toward his mother can cover his resentment and blindly blame his wife. And in collusion, the wife can continue the game and feel it is her fault that my husband is so upset. She may say to herself: "It must be my fault. I feel vague guilt, but what did I do?" Eventually she may get angry at herself and her husband for being in such a senseless bind, and consequently fulfill her husband's prophecy. The man can feel combined guilt and justification in being angry and resentful toward his wife, and the wife can feel a mixture of indignation for being treated unjustly and guilt for upsetting her husband. Reinforcing each other's mad show, both move further from the truth and the formation of a healthy community.

Other variations of interpersonal madness can involve denial and rationalization. When some of us experience behavior that is incongruent with our expectations, we simply deny the behavior. For example, young adults may be immature, but if the superiors cannot accept such behavior, they deny it. Or the superiors may rationalize—stating that their behavior is part of youth and growing up. The superiors may be parents who deny their part in their children's behavior, teachers and administrators who need student tuition, or religious who need new vocations. They can cater to and spoil youth. In turn, young adults may pretend to be clever or sincere and continue their behavior. Within themselves, however, the young adults may feel inadequate. Neither the superiors nor the youth face the truth or learn from it. Instead, they face one another with masks of madness. Such psychospiritual formation is a precarious beginning for community living.

A normal and mad strategy is to identify people with parts of themselves. For example, knowing that I have problems with anger, you identify me as simply an angry person and deny the fact that I am more than my anger. This totalizing process—identifying me simply as an angry person—gives you a sense of control over me. Furthermore, I may become more angry because you expect me to be angry or because I justifiably become angry in response to you—and, my behavior reinforces your unrealistic diagnosis.

The normal tendency to identify a person with a negative aspect, with a problem, is usually an attempt to control the other. The "totalizer" usually feels stronger than the "totalizee," though the strength is usually a compensation for underlying weakness. The totalizer gets a sense of security from controlling and not being one of "them." By focusing on the problems of others, a person can feel artificially healthy. I need not face myself and perhaps admit that I have a part in my mad community. In blaming you, I can feel artificially healthy. In seeing you as a problem I need not risk entering the mystery of your being. But mystery is the essence of any community.

Instead of maximizing, some of us minimize problems. For example, I can minimize the feelings of others until they get to me, and then I withdraw or blow up. For instance, I may refuse to admit that you are frequently angry. Even when you shout hostilely, I am apt to say, "Forget it, you don't mean it. It's just the way you are." Perhaps I cannot admit that you have problems, or that I am threatened by the truth of your anger, or that I have trouble with anger, or even all three of these ideas. Frequently, those of us who have little psychological acumen tend to minimize personal problems, often because awareness interferes with smooth functioning. We cannot or will not admit to the possibility of madness. We do not realize that emotions are modes of communication, not simply physiological reactions. Rather than admitting that you may be saying something important about both of us, I minimize and escape from the meaning in your anger and consequently miss the chance to learn from and grow with you.

When truth is pointed out, which is seldom, I will usually deny what is going on. I might say, "I really didn't mean that," or "I didn't really mean what I said." For example, when I say,

"I could kill you," I deny that there may be truth in my statement. The fact is that we can mean what we say, at least at the moment. I mean that I want to kill you at least in some ways; the words, however, "I could kill you," do not express other feelings I may also have. Under pressure of anger, I may totalize the negative side of my mixed feelings and later pretend that my ambivalence does not exist. Thus, we find ourselves coping with a tense situation.

Most of us tolerate normally mad transactions. If not directly reinforcing, we passively accept madness as long as it does not upset our lives too much or too frequently. And when my madness causes too much stress, I may be totalized, minimized, denied, warned, punished, or ostracized.

To minimize game playing, I must express all my feelings—to myself, but not necessarily to others. When I am open to myself, then I am freer to choose what to say and what course of action to take. When I am closed to myself or pretend that I am not pretending, deception, collusion, or alienation is likely to occur. This does not mean that I must rip off masks or confront because this course of action can be too threatening or violent, and consequently cause more harm than good. At a minimum I can abstain from reinforcing interpersonal games by refusing to be phony. At other times, depending on the situation (its significance and how close I am to the person(s)) and on whether I am willing to or can take the responsibility, I may take a more direct approach. For instance, my personal community would usually call for more direct and involved action than my professional community.

If I am true to myself and others, I have to be willing to take flack—to suffer for others' sake. When I go beyond normal madness, I can spontaneously intimidate people by indicting their madness. I may find that I am ignored, ridiculed, ostracized, or considered a bit mad. My integrity, however, may help me to experience and proclaim my worth. My refusal to support interpersonal games and my efforts to foster a healthy community must be based on a manifestation of love; otherwise, my life becomes painfully absurd.

No matter what kind of community I am in, I can always "dance." Though it is relatively rare for all members to live in harmony, to hear and move with the same rhythms, I can usually find someone to dance with. And if no one accepts my invitation to dance, then I may have to go outside my community, for I must never forget how to dance, not only for myself but also for others. And finally, if no one anywhere wants to dance, I can dance by myself. Though my solitary dancing may cause community flack, like "Why are you so happy?" or "Please, settle down—be normal," my dancing may eventually appeal to another to take up dancing. Perhaps such a person will first try to dance in the privacy of his or her room, and then venture out to dance together. Dancing—with life, with God, with one another—is lived community.

DRIVING PEOPLE CRAZY

One of the most effective ways of violating or destroying community is to practice normal modes of interpersonal madness that evoke abnormal madness. We normal people who live with, educate, guide, supervise, treat, or care for others can pressure them to become abnormal so that their abnormal madness can be a reaction to our normal madness. Our power to drive people crazy is especially effective when we have positions of authority such as being a parent, teacher, or superior. Reflect on these normal ways of driving people crazy.

The double bind transaction is more or less normal, though it can evoke psychopathology.[1] A double bind transaction refers to expecting and pressuring you to behave in opposite ways at the same time—to experience a contradiction. You are damned if you do and damned if you don't. For example, in the name of

1. Bateson, G., Jackson, D. D. Haley, J. and Weakland, J., *Toward a Theory of Schizophrenia*, (Behavioral Science, 1, 251, 1956).

community I may verbally pressure you to be spontaneous and warm with me, but when you do approach me, I become rigid or coldly withdraw. And when you feel hurt and rejected, I may plead innocence and ask you what is wrong with you. Being wrong in approaching or withdrawing, you (especially if you are a child, uncertain, or minimize your worth) can be very hurt and doubt your ability to cope with reality, and possibly construct your own reality. Out of painful confusion and rejection, you might withdraw, which unfortunately gives me and perhaps the community more opportunities to double bind you. Then, you might feel justifiably angry and resentful but also unnecessarily guilty so that you punish yourself and become depressed. You can then be diagnosed as unhealthy or as having problems with community living and I am considered normal. Actually both of us are mad.

Another conventional way of driving people crazy is the tangential response.[2] Here I focus on a secondary issue at the expense of what is primarily expressed; so instead of responding to what is mainly expressed, I respond to a tangent. Imagine yourself as a four-year-old child who is sent out to play while I, your parent, wax some floors. While playing you discover a worm in the mud and gleefully hurry to show me your new discovery: "Look! Look! What is this?" But I feel differently and say: "Look at your dirty feet. Go outside and wipe them off. Don't you have any idea how hard I have been working?" You feel as though the rug were pulled from under you. Feeling ashamed and hurt, you look at your worm and put your head down and walk away. Such an interaction is made because you feel confused or wrong when you are basically right, and I feel I am right when I am basically wrong. The next time you make a discovery you may be reluctant to share it and likely to keep it to yourself. And if you constantly undergo these kinds of experiences, you may learn to keep everything to yourself.

2. Ruesch, J. "The Tangential Response" In Hoch and Zuben (eds.) *Psychopathology of Communications.* New York: Grune and Stratton, 1958.

Consider a person who is manipulated psychologically. For example, I might go to a superior with honest and good intentions to complain about the superior's double standards and other unjust treatment. Instead of responding to the main issue,—the content of the protest, the superior (in family or community, in school, at work) focuses on perhaps important but nevertheless secondary feelings. The superior might say: "You feel upset about things, and it sounds like you are hurt." I might confusingly respond: "Yes, but what about your behavior. I think it's been unfair." Superior: "You feel concerned about the way I act. Maybe you should think about that, or it might be good for you to talk to a psychiatrist." Getting angry, I say: "Why? That's not what I came here for." Superior, smiling sweetly: "My dear, you seem distraught. You know I'm concerned about you." Me: "Why don't you see a psychiatrist!" Superior: "That's okay, dear, you can be angry with me, but it might be good to make sense of your feelings toward authority."

I may feel confused and hurt, angry and guilty, or helpless. The superior in the name of "care" treats me as if I have an authority problem, and I might accept the covert diagnosis or feel resentment which fulfills the superior's false prophecy. It just might be that the superior has problems with authority and with interpersonal transaction. Instead of facing the primary issues, the superior hides behind role authority and psychological techniques.

Imputing feelings to another can also be a normal and mad mode of interaction. Some of us tell others, especially people who are lower in rank or age, what and how to feel. Consider, for example, the ten-month-old who suddenly grabs the dog's bone and chews it. We might say: "Don't do that. That's not good for you. You don't like that. That's no good." The point is that the child does like and enjoys chewing on the dog's bone. Psychologically, this child's oral incorporation can be symbolic of love and affection for the dog, and besides there is usually nothing harmful in chewing on a dog's bone for a short time. Still, if you are constantly and forcefully told what and how to feel, you can learn to dislike what you really like and like what you dislike.

Telling you what you should think is equally as mad and as normal. "You really don't think that way, do you? You're not serious about that, are you?" These normal responses can pressure you to doubt yourself and to repress your convictions. I pull rank on you, and seriously believe that I can tell you what and how you should think. Instead of helping you to find the truth, I minimize your autonomy and security. Especially educators like parents and teachers, and counselors like psychotherapists and spiritual directors can foster this madness.

A similar approach is to give you answers to questions you do not have. The classic example is the child who asks where babies come from and the parents anxiously give a mini-course in the physiology of sex, even though the child would be appropriately satisfied with the answer "mommies." Giving you a solution to personal problems by listening to you for a few minutes is equally as grandiose, normal, and mad. Likewise, some of us assume there is only one way of doing things, our way, and when you do not follow our way, we punish you with physical or verbal abuse, withdrawal, ridicule, or by denying your presence.

Imposing value judgments can also be mad. Certain behavior often evokes responses like, "What's wrong? That's too bad. Why don't you try to get out of it by. . . ." For example, when you are depressed, I can consider your depression as a sign of something wrong or at best something to tolerate, and sincerely try to help you to escape from your depression. Although it may be meaningful and necessary for you to be depressed at a certain time, many of us often judge depression and similar experiences as something necessarily bad. When this is repeatedly done, you can learn to judge meaningful and necessary experiences as mad. Instead of listening to and learning from your depression, you can try to escape from your depression and consequently from yourself. With good intentions, I can actually impede growth.

Consider the dark night of spiritual growth. To experience

the absence of God, to doubt God's existence, to feel angry, depressed, and lonely are common and perhaps necessary experiences to progress spiritually. Yet I (especially if I have authority) can make you feel guilty about, repress, or numb (via work, drugs, etc.) such feelings. Or I may patronize you by praying that someday you will see the light—to be as "mature" as I. Whatever, I can at least impede and easily violate your spiritual growth.

A common and insidious way to impede psychospiritual growth is to learn "double feel." When I am put in binds, responded to tangentially, and especially have feelings and values impeding to me, I can learn to feel negatively about a feeling. I can feel depressed about being depressed, anxious about being anxious, frustrated with my frustration, and bored with my boredom. I may learn early in life to reject certain feelings, so instead of being purely depressed, I am depressed about being depressed. This is mad because much of my pain is unnecessary and actually prevents listening to what my primary depression is saying. If I could accept depression, the possibilities of making sense of my depression would be much greater. Even if explicit sense did not emerge, much wasted time and energy invested in self-rebellion would be saved. In not fighting myself, I would be freer from unnecessary pain and freer for positive experiences.

In a similar way, I can learn not to experience what I really do experience. I try to believe I am not depressed when I really am. I may tell others and myself that I had a pleasant time when in fact I was anxious and bored. I may say I am living enthusiastically, but actually I am only content. I may preach religion or say that spiritual values are important to me, but not constantly foster spiritual living.

Searles[3] analyses of driving others crazy can be considered as normal modes of interpersonal madness. The main theme is that

---

3. H. F. Searles, "The Effort to Drive the Other Person Crazy—An Element in the Etiology and Psychotherapy of Schizophrenia," *Brit. Journal of Med. Psych.*, 32, 1, (1959).

certain transactions can activate areas of a person in opposition to each other. For example, I may point out experiences that you are unaware of and that are inconsistent with your self-image. If you see yourself as a mild-mannered person and I forcefully show you that you are actually an angry person, you can feel threatened and helpless to deal with your new awareness.

Another way of driving you crazy is to stimulate you sexually in settings where gratification would be disastrous. For example, at a social gathering I am sexually suggestive and seductive and subtly stimulate you. But when we are alone, I am insulted when you become sexually aggressive. A similar method is rapidly alternating stimulation and frustration. In this case, I might be affectionate with you and when you look for more care, I become cold and withdrawn. And when you withdraw, I become affectionate again. Another way is to relate to you simultaneously on two unrelated levels. I may speak about theology and at the same time be sexually seductive. This mode of behavior can pull you in two opposite directions: the theologically theoretical and the sexually concrete. If you were to try to focus on the sexual, I could deny its existence and reprimand you as a lascivious person. Confusing? Yes—and mad.

Switching topics while maintaining the same emotional wavelength can have similar effects. I might share my feelings erotically, and then when I see you getting excited, I talk about celibate friendship while maintaining my eroticism. In this way, I can get vicarious sexual satisfaction and maintain my holy image. When these kinds of interpersonal relationships occur, we can behave as if the ability to discern the true meaning of experience is lost. Or we can become hyper cautious or feel pressured to hurt in return.

These and other normal ways of driving one another crazy certainly do not foster healthy growth in self or in marital, religious, or single community living. Instead, they impede, violate, and can destroy our destiny—to grow in love. Our first step is to admit our potential to play these lethal games and to be responsible when we do play them. Then our challenge is to stop and respond in love.

✳ ✓   But what can we do when we interact with respect while others try to drive us crazy? It is too tempting and easy to respond the same way, to be hostile, or to play the martyr role in hopes that the other feels guilty. We can first realize what is happening and try to understand, though not condone, their behavior. Then one of our most difficult and truest tests is to respond in love—to accept, confront, and transcend madness. When our love is rejected or passed by, it is very difficult to continue to love, but love is our hope and saving grace. In love madness may continue, but in love there is more than madness.

COUNTERFEITS OF LOVE

Some of our most subtle forms of interpersonal madness are the counterfeits of love. Since love is usually considered an essential dynamic of being healthy and happy with oneself and in community, madness disguised as love can be especially destructive. Consider some of these modes of "love"—of mad community—that actually impede and can destroy love—the essence of psychospiritual growth.

Although love often includes kindness, love and kindness are not identical—and, kindness can be contrary to love. When I am kind, I am benevolent, just, and gentle and try to abstain from the rough and indifferent. Kindness, however, can be a mode of madness when it is primarily a function of altruism and expediency. I can be altruistic because it is the easiest way to protect myself from responsibility, confrontation, or anxiety.

For example, I can be concerned about everybody except my own community. Being a lover of humanity, I escape from my main responsibility—my community—by being overly involved with social concerns. I "love" everybody except those I should: While I save the world, my community (including myself) perishes. Or I could be a superior who when confronted with criticism smiles sweetly and withdraws. Though I may have good intentions, I hide behind a mask of kindness instead of facing and responding to the issue.

I may find kind behavior as a clever way to manipulate people or to gain affection and approval. I constantly act like a sensitive sales person: With kindness I try to sell my product—myself. I may give "positive strokes" and "warm fuzzies" that may make some people feel good. My concern for others is actually concern for myself. Although I seem nice, I am exploitive—even if my manipulative concern is said to be for the good of the patient, the community's welfare, or done in the name of God.

Kind acts can also be condescending. When I say to you, "you're nice," my comment can be about a relatively unimportant trait of your personality. Although saying that you are nice can sound kind, it can also be a way of disguising deeper truths. Sometimes it is necessary to point out things that are unkind. To tell you thoughtfully that you are arrogant can show genuine concern, (or it can also be an arrogant way of hurting you). I can hide behind the mask of kindness rather than face a difficult situation. My saccharine smile, timid acceptance, and silent withdrawals may blur the truth, impede growth, and evoke ambivalent resentment. Sometimes it is easier to be "kind" than loving.

We can also be altruistic do-gooders who are usually kind to people from a lower class: The "rich" are kind to the "poor," the "intelligent" to the "dumb," the "healthy" to the "unhealthy," and the "wise" to the "unwise." "We' are kind to "them." Though we are kind, we need not be loving; in fact, our kindness can be a disguise for authentic love. Being mad givers of kindness, we try to force the endurers of kindness to feel lower and to look up to us, and we feel "good" because we are helping the "less fortunate." Actually, we "fortunate" lovers convey that we are better than the "unfortunate." Our kindness is for ourselves—to gain recognition, to undo guilt, or to be a success. And our madness breeds resentment, estrangement, and separation.

If I have high ideals, especially spiritual ones, and I am not growing in my marital, religious, or single vocation, I may feel even more urged to help the weak, low, and inferior so that I can feel strong, high, and superior. My social concerns and service may be compensations for my spiritual failures. Besides, I can get social recognition and rewards for my "outstanding service." Though my frontstage performance of madness may gain applause, my backstage life stagnates in silent boredom and emptiness.

Healthy kindness emerges from healthy love. Lovers find kindness a major way to show their love. Paradoxically, when loving we stand on the common ground of love and feel the union of being two in one. When we are genuinely concerned, we try to be considerate, warm, and gentle. We realize that kind acts can express and promote love.

Life offers daily opportunities to be kind in love. The very fact that we are radically imperfect and more or less mad—one of a kind—demands kindness; otherwise, we would be constantly frustrated, hurt, or embarrassed. To focus on positive rather than negative qualities of others can be kind. To accept unkind or hostile behavior, to respect another's privacy, to ask thoughtfully if we can help, can be kind. Kindness in community involves and engenders perspective in "the" present and hope for the future. To visit the sick, to show delight with the elderly, to remember the forgotten can be kind. Never to take people for granted but to appreciate them is love in action.

Too many of us deceive ourselves into thinking that giving is necessarily good, but giving can also be a mode of madness. For example, I may always pay for meals, throw parties, and buy gifts to indebt and control you. I may not give for your sake but for my own. And you can give me gifts to ameliorate your feelings of indebtedness, to even the score, and to free yourself from my control. If I treat a friend or spouse unjustly, I might give them a gift mainly to relieve my guilt, not to ask for forgiveness and reconciliation. Instead of admitting my injustice and sharing myself, I try to hide behind my gifts, buy them off, and perhaps make them feel guilty. Or I may give only to receive: I will give and do anything as long as I get an equal return, and as soon as

I am no longer given to, I stop giving. For instance, I love only if you love me; when you reject, withdraw from, or are indifferent to my love, I stop loving. Actually, my motive is self-satisfaction, not your welfare. In these "loving" transactions, I am actually a taker, not a healthy giver. Although my interpersonal relationships may be normal and seem loving, I am mad.

We can also give as a way of hiding ourselves. We give things instead of ourselves—presents instead of personal presence. As parents we can give everything to our children except ourselves, and consequently raise ambivalent, hurt, and resentful children. Our mad struggle for success and recognition can leave little time and room for personal care. Our children become members of a hassled generation—fully satisfied but empty.

Giving is good when it is for the other's sake. Giving things, time, and effort can be manifestations of genuine concern and to use things authentically can be a celebration of life. But when I give my teenager a car instead of time and a trip instead of understanding, I am mad. When I give a friend a glib remark instead of a concerned response, I violate our friendship. When I give a perfunctory blessing instead of a loving glance, I promote resentment. I hide behind my giving and promote alienation rather than intimacy.

Some of us still feel that we must like a person in order to love. We like certain qualities in another because they bring personal meaning. Unlike liking, love is not totally contingent upon satisfaction, affirmation, and fun but on genuine concern that includes the opposite of these and other experiences.

Loving and liking, however, can be related and influence the kind of love we have for one another. I can love and consequently be civil and kind to someone I dislike intensely, though I would not befriend or spend much time with that person. If I felt I had to like in order to love, I would drive myself mad. Or if I felt I had to be equally intimate with everyone in my religious community, my struggle to share would at least cause serious tension. Though I cannot be a friend with everyone, I can be friendly. We sometimes forget that a religious or similar community is not a family. On the other hand, although I like a friend, I always experience something to dislike. There is always something about everyone that is irritating and uncomfortable. It is good to keep in mind that we would really not love anyone if our love depended totally on what we liked.

Indifference is in many ways the most fatal violation of love. When I am indifferent, I have no feelings for or against you as a person. One kind of indifference occurs when I do not recognize any aspect of you. I act as though you do not exist, and therefore you make no positive or negative impact on me. I pass you by. I am mad because I do not recognize who you are—a person of infinite worth. My behavior does not include a minimum of respect and justice, but I carelessly do not care at all.

We can consciously take care not to care. I can give people the "ice water treatment" by not talking or responding to them. I make an effort to pretend that they do not exist, that their presence does not matter. Perhaps this is the worst treatment to accept. Frequent reasons for being indifferent in this way are personal hurt (having been insulted, misunderstood, unappreciated), jealousy, envy, and felt indifference. Whatever the reason, such indifference violates love.

More often we can be indifferent without conscious intent. In any age and especially in our age of future shock, technocracy, workism, etc., we can too easily take others for granted. Particularly when people are quiet (perhaps temperamentally), sell themselves short, or do not know how to take initiative, we can treat them like furniture. Though we may live or work with them, they are not recognized and appreciated for what they can do and especially for who they are. We forget them and pass them by. It may be good for us to take a second look, daily, at the people we work and live with. They are just as human as we are.

I can also practice a type of indifference wherein I am mainly interested in the function that you can perform. I deny you personhood and totalize you as a function. For example, when

I experience a waitress merely as a waitress—an impersonal function, I treat her efficiently and coldly. I treat her as if she were a robot whose only value lies in her function to serve me. Seeing and using her only in terms of her functionality is mad. Although I should not encounter her intimately, I can focus on her service with a caring disposition. Although the situation is primarily functional, it can also have consideration and warmth.

Think of the nurse and doctor who see the patient merely as sick and are indifferent to personhood. They treat the patient as an impaired function and minimize and insult the patient as a person. They should be interested not only in the person's illness but also in the person who has the illness. Good nurses and doctors know that their personal concern is as important as their functional treatment. A nurse who is scared to care and must be totally objective breeds resentment and impedes healing. And her job soon becomes insipid, boring, and sheer resistance. Treatment without care is technological barbarism that financially and socially supports madness.

When we communicate in madness, we avoid responsibility— our ability to respond to what is really going on. By covering instead of uncovering the truth, we minimize our freedom and avoid decisions. We want to maintain ourselves within the confines of normal madness and to avoid the pain that may be necessary for a creative breakthrough to healthy communication and community.

Almost all of us engage more or less and at times in normally mad transactions. How often we play these games and how much we depend on them, however, primarily determine our degree of madness. Our negative transactions need not do much harm and can even help us become healthier. For example, my periodic indifference can challenge me to be thoughtful and friendly or my tendency to impute feelings may help me to listen more openly to others. Too frequently, however, we simply learn to live with madness and fail to learn from and purge it.

When we become more mad, we become progressively estranged from whole living. We frustrate ourselves and cheat others, and we can too easily miss important experiences. We can live in a community that is fraught with games, alienation, and pain—a community that fails to nourish at-homeness and growth. Although our lives make some sense, our search for meaning incorporates needless difficulties that shackle the possibilities of becoming. We can become estranged from the paramount loci of love—persons. Life on earth is too short to go through such motions of living. We can struggle to grow together in love.

CHAPTER FIVE

Moments of Madness

"Sometimes I don't know what gets into me. I can get so angry that I don't know what to do—scream? Shake someone? Tell them where to get off? Argue? Fight? What do I do? I usually hold it in and feel miserable. What else can I do? If I express my anger, I usually feel worse afterwards.

"As a matter of fact, you could say that I get mad at myself for being mad. Though I don't like what's happening, I don't like getting angry either. What good is there in being angry. It's not good, is it?"

A lot of us may feel similar to this person. We may have much difficulty in making positive sense of our anger, and perhaps feel guilty for being angry. We find ourselves getting angry, then guilty, then mad at ourselves. Too often, we either explode or implode rather than behave constructively. Normally we feel that anger excludes love.

There are times when we have experiences that do not seem to make much sense and that seem to make matters worse. Rather than promoting mad life-styles or transactions, we can have moments of normal madness. These mad moments, however, are not rewarded as some mad life styles are, nor are they accepted like mad transactions. Instead, moments of madness are feelings and/or actions that are more often tolerated or eventually rejected, but nevertheless are part of normal living. When we have mad moments, such as being hostile, we are neither considered abnormally mad nor are we incarcerated. Yet such behavior is seldom socially sanctioned, and it can be painfully disruptive to personal growth. Let us reflect on the sense and nonsense of some of our mad times.

ANGER

Although anger is normal and can be healthy, it can cause us much guilt and conflict. Common negative injunctions like: "Don't get angry," or angrily shouting at someone: "I have had enough. Be quiet, damn it!" Or people withdraw from us or fight us when we get angry. Too infrequently is anger okay and positive. Instead, we tend to feel that anger is necessarily mad and bad.

Anger is a mode of aggression that says "No." When I am angry, I do not like what is happening. I may be frustrated, dislike something, or feel hurt. Whatever the reason, I want something to stop or change. For instance, if you pull rank on me or treat me as second class, I am likely to feel angry. My feelings might say: "You have no right treating me this way. You are hurting me. I have the right to be treated with at least the minimum of respect and justice."

Anger can be a *no* that is in service of a more basic *yes*. To say *no* to unjust treatment can be an affirmation of my own dignity, and I might help you to think about acting justly. Thus, anger can be a healthy and necessary way to maintain and promote justice. Instead of being violent or hostile, anger can be a strong, firm, and direct way of improving a situation. Indeed, anger can be an articulation of love.

Anger in itself is neither healthy or mad, good or bad, but how we act on anger primarily determines its value. And unfortunately we can act madly toward our anger.

A mad mode of anger occurs when I explode in anger. Often because I feel anger is bad, I repress it or "let it build up" until I explode or "dump on" someone. Instead of listening to what my anger is saying when it initially occurs and freely choose how to act, I fail to listen and postpone direct action until I become as volatile as a powder keg that is ready to explode.

Furthermore, when I explode, I often transfer anger that has accumulated from any situations to one situation so that my angry response is inappropriate—"too much." And we often displace anger on those we love, for we feel that they will not reject or withdraw from us as others might. Or we might displace our pent-up anger on helpless creatures like children and animals or perhaps on anyone who has less power and status than we.

Such explosive behavior is mad. We neither behave justly nor do we improve the situation. We are more likely to hurt unnecessarily and to cover instead of uncover the truth. Destructive anger militates against healthy and holy growth, for it is not integrated with love.

Rather than exploding, some of us "implode." Perhaps because I have learned that anger is bad or because I fear being rejected or hurt, I hold my anger in and beat myself for being angry. My implosiveness is often accompanied with withdrawal so that when I get angry, I hold my feelings inside myself and withdraw from people. Instead of acting constructively, I treat myself and others unfairly and destructively. Though I am unfair to others, I am most destructive to myself. My pent-up anger can make me feel on edge and tired—precariously beat, and my anger may cause psychosomatic illness such as an ulcer or hypertension.

Actually all anger should be expressed—to myself but not necessarily to others. When I can listen to and learn from my anger, then I can more freely choose the appropriate time and way to act on my anger, and sometimes no explicit action is the best action. In anger I can try to do what is best for the situation, which may mean confrontation, disagreement, criticism, or withdrawal.

Another way anger can be mad is when it leads to "totalization" or blind anger. Especially when I am not open to what my anger expresses, I can identify you with what makes me angry. For instance, if you do not listen to me and take me for granted, I might get understandably angry. But if I see you *only* as a nonlistening, closed person, then I am being unfair. Even though you may consistently be closed, you are much more than a nonlistening person. To identify whole persons with their problems is mad, for it denies other realities and precludes growth.

Anger often evokes anger, explosive or implosive, that is mainly destructive retaliation rather than constructive reconciliation. When someone hurts us fairly (by expressing truth that we deny) or unfairly (by treating us as less than we are), we tend to hurt back—to even the score: zere to zero. At this point, anger often turns into violence—a mad experience.

VIOLENCE

When violent, I attempt to destroy your experience—physically, psychologically, or spiritually. For instance, physical violence can include the destruction of property and the physical mutilation or murder of another person. And some of us can be physically violent in the name of honesty, truth, and love. Think of children who are unjustly beaten for "their own good" or innocent people killed in the service of peace.

Psychological violence often takes the form of driving people crazy. For example, in the double bind situation, the "loving" parent is violent when harassing a child into being non-violent or when coldly demanding that the child be warmly respectful. Such mad communication can confuse the child's perception of reality and teach the child to be afraid of and distant to others. And more normal madness can be perpetuated because the parent's violence promotes just anger in the child, and when the anger is expressed, the child gets attacked—which then may turn into hostility. Of course, such violence can occur between adults especially when one has authority. Though we may deplore physical violence, we may be unaware of our psychological violence.

I am violent when I manipulate or exploit you. If I am a disciple of powerism, for instance, I am violent when I use others as a means to my own end. With little or no care, I handle people as if they were tools needed to complete a task. I demand that people support and serve me. Or I may wear a mask of benevolence and concern to control people. Or when I say, "What's wrong, can't you take a stand?" I may mean: "I will not accept you unless you take my stand."

Spiritual violence is most destructive because what a person holds most sacred is destroyed. This violence undermines the ground on which a person stands and promotes a meaningless life. For example, we are violent when we seduce and exploit each other sexually in the name of love. We repress and escape from love by pretending our exclusively genital encounter is love. This madness does not only occur between single people but perhaps more frequently in marriage. We can pretend to legitimatize via marriage the evasion of authentic love by giving it a formal appearance of normality. We have the permission to destroy our marriage in good form. Violent madness also occurs when we reject, scorn, or are indifferent to another's love. A person can be spiritually wounded by being violently hurt in love.

Being violently mad, I can be like a pressure cooker, ready to strike out with physical, psychological, or spiritual violence. Being "on top" of others—ridiculing, criticizing, blaming them, brings me some sense of security, and when threatened, I become especially violent. Actually I am weak because a certain kind of environmental stress automatically evokes violence in me and because my violent style is often compensation for feelings of inadequacy. Although I may be talented and normal, I feel inadequate and desperately try to make others feel as small or smaller. When something like alcohol weakens my control, everyone may be fair game. When not threatened, I may be kind and considerate and often guilty and repentent for past explosions.

I can understand that my extreme and inappropriate behavior often occurs because I impulsively transfer pent-up feelings from the past toward people in the present. My rage is actually directed at many people, past and present, at the same time. If I hold my feelings in, I am more likely to explode (or implode and become tense). And if I repress violence toward others like my mother and sisters, I may overly react toward my wife. In interpersonal relationships I feel tenuously okay as long as there is support and affirmation, but when threatened, I become violent to protect myself from present and past pain. As time goes on, I alienate others and can eventually end up alone.

I must be careful not to be violent toward my violence. Instead of taking a mad approach toward my madness, I can try to have the strength and humility to listen to my violent feelings. What am I violent for? Do I really feel inferior? Am I envious? Am I hurt? Am I still seeking revenge for something that happened decades ago? Even if I do not discover the reasons for my violence, I can still foster non-violent behavior.

I can take special care to be kind and gentle. Instead of overpowering people, I can be quiet and listen to them. Before disagreeing or leveling them, I can affirm the truth in what they say. I can stand back instead of rushing in. I can reflect on what violence does to others and to myself. I can ask myself if I really want to be violent and if I have to be. Can I show respectful concern especially when violence emerges within me?

HOSTILITY

When I am hostile, I experience you as an enemy to hurt and/or defend against. My aggression is ready to lash out at you—to wound you and make you back off. Standing in hostility, I can be tense and on edge, perhaps suspicious and hypersensitive to any possible threat like criticism. Although some hostile people are abnormal like the psychotic paranoid person, I am normal. I do not create and act on delusions of grandeur and persecution to the extent that I am too disruptive and institutionalized. Being in normal formation, I keep the standards of normalcy and am more or less tolerated.

A particularly mad consequence is to interpret almost everything in terms of my framework and consequently fail to understand anyone who disagrees with me. Because I am too insecure to open myself to another's view, I must carefully hold on to what I have. And I have difficulty in praising anyone because I identify you as an enemy and perhaps because I see your success or personality as a threat to me. For example, I may covertly spy on you to keep up with or to criticize you. Instead of sharing your happiness and success, I focus on your imperfections.

Actually, I am injured and weak, and my hostility can be a defense and a cover for underlying inadequacy. Since I am insecure, I must constantly prove and protect myself. I feel that I will hurt you before you hurt me. Consider, for instance, hostility towards a friend. I can usually accept compliments, views that dovetail with my own, and in general non-threatening conversation. But when I feel insecure, I become hostile not so much to hurt my friend but to prove and protect myself. Although I can be friendly and relatively loose when feeling securely in control, I feel I must be on guard so others will not get the best of me. I am normally paranoid in that I experience others as real or potential enemies whom I must guard against or attack before they attack me. When things are not going my way, I may fight or withdraw, or fight and then withdraw. But behind my aggressive defense, I feel painfully weak and scared.

Many of us may have much difficulty listening to our hostility and consequently express it indirectly. If I am such a person, my hostility is ambiguously and ambivalently covert, and consequently you have difficulty in dealing with me; you seldom know where and how you stand with me. When you confront me, I deny that I am hostile and may even try to make you look hostile. For example, I may not like you reading a novel, but instead of telling you directly, I try to make fun of you or embarrass you while you are reading. I might say: "What are you doing?" "Some people seem to have all the time." "I wish someone would help with the work around here." "Is that all you have to do?" When you ask what I am mad about I say: "Oh, I'm not mad. Why do you ask? Are you mad?" Furthermore, such passively hostile behavior usually evokes the same behavior. So you might respond, "Because you seem so overjoyed with my reading." Thus, we reinforce each other and increase the likelihood of more passively hostile behavior.

This kind of hostile transaction reinforces mutual manipulation and exploitation. Instead of honestly facing each other, we hide our hostility behind masks of competent coercion. Instead of speaking the truth (at least to ourselves), we present gifts of violence wrapped with concern. In pretending to be what we are not, we hide from and violate each other. In such transactions, it is relatively easy (though not healthy) to return hostility, to withdraw, or to evoke guilt—ways to violate communal and self growth. To be helpful and healthy takes courage, concern, and compassion.

Part of my difficulty may be that I feel that if I admit my hostility (even to myself), I will be worthless and rejected. Although I need and want love, I feel I will lose or destroy love if I am hostile. I often hate being in such a bind but feel helpless in admitting to my hostility, or hate myself for being hostile. Thus, I may try to compromise: to be hostile and non-hostile at the same time.

I can admit that hostility constricts and tends to destroy experience. When I am hostile, I hurt others. And when people are hurt, they are usually inclined to be hostile or to withdraw, and if they are continually hurt, they usually withdraw from me and I soon find myself alienated. Though I may make your life miserable, the most miserable life is my own.

When hostile, I can feel guilty and depressed because I broke a law or because of my fear of being rejected, and also because I was unjust to, hurt, and hindered a person. I can listen to my unsettling feeling to learn to behave better and strive to make creative restitution. How can I do this constructively? I may not always say that I am sorry, but I make up, in some way, for the harm I have done. I do something for the person I have wounded: I come back from my hostile moments to care more deeply. My hostility can challenge me to build community.

Hostility calls for hospitality.[1] Instead of identifying myself or you with hostility, I give us room to be more than just hostile. Though I accept hostility, I invite myself and others to be wholly present. Courage is called for because hostility often means that we may be deeply hurt. I may have learned early in life to distrust people and to hurt and control them so they are less likely to hurt me. I try to build strong and aggressive positions that protect weakness, compensate for insecurity, and hide pain. Instead of using hostility to destroy life, I must accept hostility as a painful way to see myself and others more deeply. If I can courageously be hospitable with my own hostility, I open the doors for understanding and healthy growth. In the house of love hostility can be taken wholeheartedly and healed.

HATE

Hate, another mode of violence, is a form of mad care whereby I take care to cripple or destroy you. In hate I try to paralyze your freedom and personhood. I no longer want to understand you and often try to make your existence miserable. My stand is to wipe out your stand. I say to you: "Since I cannot stand you, I want to destroy your stand." Hate is psychospiritual murder. For example, consider marriages (or any community) that apparently begin in love but often end in hate. Instead of promoting each other's welfare, we learn to impede and violate each other. We eventually feel we cannot stand living with each other, and we separate in order not to kill one another.

There can be many reasons why I hate you. For instance, you might disrupt my life, evoke unacceptable experiences, or elicit guilt. I might hate what you stand for so that your existence is a threat to my own. For example, I might hate you because you are living a better life. Your style of living is so irritating that I look for reasons to criticize, scandalize, and "kill" you.

---

1. Henri J. Nouwen, *The Wounded Healer: Ministry in Contemporary Society:* (Garden City, N. Y.: Doubleday, 1972).

Often we hate because we are painfully hurt. Being hurt in love can cripple me for life. Past love turns to hate so that my desire is to make you a corpse that can no longer hurt me. For example, a girl may try to love her father, but when he exploits, rejects, or ignores her, she feels hurt, cheated, and resentful. A lethal danger is that her hurt and hate may spread to all men.

We also have to be aware of cultural pressures that can inhibit the expression of love and increase the tendency to hate. Although we talk about love and play love roles, seldom is authentic love culturally promoted. We can, however, be culturally conditioned to take hate for granted. Since our threshold for hate is higher, we can incorporate more hate so that when we express our hate, we are more destructive.

Consider a more subtle form of hate—finding togetherness in hating others. Our "love" is grounded on the promise of two people hating a third person. If "we" would not be against "them," we would lose our togetherness. Though we are basically at odds with someone, we come together when we talk about a mutual enemy. Although we feel together in hate, we actually do violence to each other in the guise of a good relationship. Our "loving hate" is a popular form of madness.

Hate (demonic) and love (divine) can, however, be seen as similar experiences. Dissimilar to disliking and liking, hate and love are not directed towards this or that quality but toward the whole person. The hateful person wants to destroy another's existence, and a loving person wants to promote existence. Furthermore, hate emergent from jilted love can be the deepest and most "authentic" form of hate. In such hate, I may be close to love, for it seems that if only you would say "yes" to me, hate would cease. I seem to have no course but to love or hate. It is understandable from my perspective that I would hate because I feel my existence is being destroyed and to keep some dignity, I feel I have to destroy the one who rejected me. My spirit of creation is transformed to a demonic power of destruction.

To turn hate to love, I must honestly ask myself what I hate for. Does my hate hide hurt? Can I admit that my hate can be used as a powerful weapon to protect my vulnerable self? I can also realize that I can intensely dislike what some people do, but still love them. Even though I cannot stand them, I can stand for them. I try to do the best I can for them, which may mean staying out of their way unless called to act differently. I strive to love no matter what—even in the midst of hate.

HISTRIONICS

Some of us tend to be histrionic. Especially when anxious, we interact in an intense, dynamic, and exciting way. We cannot stand the mundane and everyday but want every experience to be a peak experience. In our interpersonal relations we can be highly emotional and outgoing. For instance, when introduced to me, I may act as if I have known you for years, and I get close and chummy too quickly. I seem to be smothering you with care. Especially when under stress, I am likely to gush over you—suffocating you with my dynamic presence.

From a distance, I appear to be full of life; on closer inspection, however, my vitalism can be seen to be a mask that betrays underlying fear and depression. For example, I may constantly talk about love and perhaps be loving, but at a certain point I withdraw. I play a dramatic role of love and may actually be afraid of lasting and responsible love. Living only in the "now"— cut off from the past and future, I want permanent fulfillment instantly and without risks. I am a good candidate for feelism, especially "love movements" where virtually everybody loves everybody (except people who dislike me) and where everything is shared. My love, however, can be more phony than authentic. I hide behind masks of love.

I can be skilled at playing roles for approving applause. For example, I might behave as the suffering saint for attention and affection. People (who usually do not live with me) may like and feel sorry for me because of my intense and sincere mode of living. Actually, I may be covertly protecting myself from being totally rejected. Simply being present or standing up for my rights is too threatening because I feel that I am not good enough. Instead of giving or proclaiming myself, I give performances that evoke approval and protect me.

Or I can play the classical poor soul who is always low and tired, lacks enthusiasm and a sense of enjoyment, and is prone to be a martyr. Although I try to be vital, I always seem to apologize for not being quite able to make it. And I might console myself in knowing that my suffering will get me a "high place in heaven."

To cut through my sincere madness, I have to claim my fringe benefits. For example, I may get attention and pity and I may pat myself on the back for being such a good guy. My primary gain can be withdrawing from the risk and responsibility of being myself. I would rather be nursed and pitied. I can be an excellent candidate for "momism." I have to be careful of marrying a woman who feels sorry for me, tells me what to do, and praises and punishes me. When I want something, I just yell to my wife, "Hey Mom..." My real mother and wife can be basically the same in that they support and promote my behavior. Or I may be a celibate priest who hires, befriends, and depends on a housekeeper who pampers and spoils me. Or I may be a docile and suffering wife whom relatives and neighbors feel sorry for. They wonder how I can put up with such an insensitive husband. Or I may be a nun who unconsciously encourages exploitation and general abuse from authorities, and then I complain with tears. I should discern whether I am putting myself on the floor and unknowingly inviting people to walk on me. I may be afraid to stand up for my dignity—to risk confronting people with angry love.

WITHDRAWAL

Many of us can have mad moments of withdrawal. We can be prone to withdraw from uncomfortable and threatening situations. We may also interact in a distant and opaque way and withdraw from straight and especially close relationships to avoid the risk of being known. We seldom express our inner feelings or let our insides out. We can withdraw personally, so one meets a body without spirit. If I am such a person, I can be written off as eccentric, snobbish, or shy, but people seldom realize that my objectivity and distance are ways of protecting myself. Actually, I usually want to share myself, but I am scared of being hurt.

Although I can usually function efficiently and productively—normally, I may seldom show and give my inner self. I can be a good candidate for workism and powerism, or I can become a "machine man" who operates smoothly but who fails to be intimate. Western culture, moreover, supports withdrawn tendencies by overvaluing functionality at the expense of spirituality. That is, transrational and intimate experiences are not supported socially or subsidized as is rational and technical behavior. As long as I function normally, people usually do not care what is going on inside me. Unless I disrupt their functioning, they usually let me alone.

Being normal and withdrawn, I may be highly successful and mad because personal feelings can be put aside in service of efficiency. I can become competent with things but cold with people. Although I may be skilled at coping with tasks, my presence to others is shallow and superficial. Splitting my inner and outer lives, people meet the surface of my personality and experience a fragmented person. In certain situations, like drinking, my inner self may come out, often aggressively or depressively. Failing to love, I can even become a caricature of a spiritual person. Though I preach love, I seldom give love. As I grow older, I feel more empty and hollow and feel that something is missing in life. Something is missing: myself in love.

Often I am timid and tense and really do not know how to get my insides out. Though I feel warmth and love within myself, I may appear relatively cold and indifferent. Actually I may not know how to initiate conversation or I may feel inadequate when I have nothing to say. Most often, I sell myself terribly short, and in minimizing myself I risk maximizing the other. I work on the assumption that no one would be genuinely interested in such a worthless person. Consequently, I withdraw and my spirit starves for love.

I may try to withdraw from all interpersonal relationships, especially intimate ones, and rather than having mad times, I lead a mad life. As long as I am by myself, dealing with things or perhaps interacting with animals and nature, I feel okay. I can function at work and in everyday living as long as I do not have to be personally involved with people. I reject invitations to be intimate because I fear being rejected myself, and I defend against closeness often because I feel unworthy to be touched.

We have seen, however, that not all withdrawal is mad. Sometimes it is necessary and good to withdraw. When I withdraw from a hostile or boring group, I may be acting in the best interests of self and the group. Or I may withdraw in solitude to listen to and to reflect on life. Mad withdrawal usually means that I will not or cannot face what is happening because of weakness or threat. Instead of truthfully admitting to my experience, I hide behind asocial behavior.

Although my mad withdrawal may seem safe and protect me from immediate hurt, it can progressively destroy me. I can find myself using more time and energy trying to abstain from social and especially intimate relations that are necessary for me to grow. I may even find myself hiding behind false selves that mask and protect the real me, and eventually not know how to show and share my true self.

It is necessary for me to risk being hurt in intimacy. Of course, I should not share myself indiscriminately, but when justly called for. To think that I can share equally to all people or even to all of my community is dangerous and impossible, but I can share (which includes listening and free withdrawal) in various ways to various people.

When I feel stuck, perhaps neither in nor out—in a nowhere

land, it is often helpful to discover how I may have been hurt
and what I am afraid of. I may discover that I never had much
opportunity to be intimate and that closeness was repressed in
my environment. Or I may uncover that on several occasions
I was close to a person who eventually rejected me. Whatever,
I may see that I no longer have to relive past patterns of behavior.

To be with another I must also be open to myself. Paradoxically, solitude is one of the best ways to learn to be with and
to be for another. In solitude, I strive to claim and embrace myself.
Being present and true to myself gives me courage to be with
others.

I cannot willfully choose to be intimate but I can put myself
in situations where intimacy is more likely to occur. In social and
more personal gatherings I can try to show more of my whole
self instead of hiding myself. I can listen to and especially see
that others are basically the same as I. People, no matter how
"actualized and dynamic" they seem to be, are decidedly imperfect with problems, limits, and fears. When I can really see
them in me and I in them, I can begin to show and share myself
more personally. Especially in situations like play and love I can
try to let go and "come out."

DEPENDENCY

We can be normal persons who may find ourselves willing to
do anything as long as we get what we want. Such parasitic tendencies are fraught with neediness, and like an infant I take but
do not give unconditionally. In such a situation, I see you primarily in terms of need satisfaction so that I am dependent on you
to feed me. Without your food I feel I will starve to death.
Without your affirmation, I am worthless. Yet I also resent people for being higher and stronger than I, for having so much
power over me. Consequently, people experience my sweet
behavior with caution—and for good reason because when someone does not meet my expectations, I can become hostile, usually

passively and sometimes explosively, or I feel hurt and apologize profusely. Thus, I am in a bind: I hate what I need and need what I hate.

Consider dependent propensities in a dating situation. A woman may initially like my milquetoast behavior, but she soon gets irritated with my passivity, like always asking her what she wants to do, waiting on her, and seldom taking initiative. She feels uncomfortable with my constant leaning, and when she gets angry, I plead innocent. How would such a nice guy be guilty of this? The woman may feel guilty and foolish for being seduced. Eventually, the relationship ends, and I can look for another breast to suck.

If I let my dependent tendencies get out of hand, I can be an excellent candidate for momism. I may marry a woman who mothers me and expect her to cater to me, to give unconditionally, to be always available—to feed, clothe, and comfort me. When I give to her, I demand a return. And if I am too frustrated or hurt, I can always run home to mommy.

If I am unmarried or my wife refuses to mother me, I can be successful in creating a mother inside myself—a maternal alter ego. When weak, scared, hurt, or need, I can support, comfort, sympathize, and nourish myself. And I can scream, pout, demand, and pressure women or men to satisfy my needs or to make them feel confused, angry, or guilty. I expect and demand that others appreciate, nourish, and affirm me; otherwise, I get hurt, become angry, and/or withdraw.

Or I can be an obsequious woman who follows "dadism." I can marry a man whom I look up to and divinize; I see and treat him as the all perfect daddy who will always affirm and comfort me. Part of my madness is that I sell myself short and I may subtly control my husband by putting him on a pedestal. Actually, my husband cannot move very much on his precarious perch, and I am unfair to him because like any person he is far from perfect.

I can admit that expecting him to be perfect affords me comfort and control.

Though not necessarily unhealthy, dependent relationships are more or less normally mad and consequently impede healthy growth. Being dependent I minimize my worth and overestimate your worth. Consequently, I not only cheat myself (and lose or hide my dignity), but also I cheat you from learning from and appreciating me. Though I can still be a good person, my dependency limits my spirit so that I am afraid to move or be as free as I possibly can. Feeling boxed in, I find it too difficult to breathe, and though my spirit does not suffocate to death, my breathing is often unnecessarily labored.

Do I really have to make people better than I? Can I catch myself maximizing another and minimizing myself and see what is actually happening. Must I seek attention and affirmation from others rather than affirming myself. Must I do this? Can I see more alternatives and try to act on them? If I cannot move, what stops me? Does my history tell me something about the dependent me? Can I say yes to myself no matter what and consequently affirm others?

My challenge is to become an autonomous person—to freely choose to be interdependent. With myself and others I must realize that I am a person of worth and that my life is mainly in my hands, not in others. Others cannot give me meaning (though they can help me find it), nor can they live my life for me. Only I can live my life. My tendencies toward dependency can be opportunities for autonomy.

Knowing that I can consciously exploit others, I can be motivated to take a charitable rather than parasitic posture. Instead of being hyperdependent, I can strive to freely give and be interdependent. I can treat others with unconditioned respect—neither divinizing nor demonizing them. I try to transcend my need for people satisfying my needs, and I strive to actualize my call to love people unconditionally.

COMPULSIVENESS

Some of us can be normal but have compulsive tendencies that may be moments of madness or opportunities for growth. If I am inclined to be compulsive, I must be careful, for I tend to want to have everything in a certain order and everyone to act a certain way. I dislike leaving loose ends, not finishing a task, finishing late, or in general—imperfection. The way to think and to do things is my way—and, I may consciously and unconsciously pressure people to agree with or at least follow my approach. Although I may not intentionally manipulate and exploit people, I can control people with rigidity. Being inhibited, too conscientious, and domineering, I can seldom relax and be spontaneous. When I do forget myself and let go, I soon feel embarrassed and return to my rigid ways.

Picture this profile of a normal but compulsive mother. Her house is always spotless: The living room is for show, not for living; toys are kept in a box, not played with; everything is covered to prevent dirt; and you must keep off the grass. Life is a strict schedule: Meals are always at a certain time; Monday is for washing and Friday is for cleaning; bedtime is always the same time; there are set times for work, play, eating, sleeping. Feelings are overly restricted: Her body is rigid; smiling is an effort; play is a task; spontaniety is rare; and sex is frigid. Thinking is narrow and stale. Her way is the right way for everyone; creativity is nill; linear approaches are dominant; and speech is aggressive, choppy, and colorless. Her husband, who is often dependent, lives with it. And her children can easily grow rigid and resentful.

Some of us in reaction against such a compulsive and legalistic background try to go to the opposite extreme. For instance, we seldom enforce rules and keep things in place, and we may allow our children to do what they want. Although our situation may initially look free and open, we can unknowingly impede healthy growth. Our children can become selfish and spoiled people who have little concern for others and who lack discipline to be free. They may live with the assumption that all needs should and must be satisfied—that discomfort makes no sense. They can learn to expect that life owes them something or to take life for granted.

Our compulsivity is often rooted in our past. Many of us grew up in an environment and culture that was legalistic and that lacked healthy expression of feelings. In some of our homes, anger that fostered fear was mainly expressed and seldom was affection manifested. Also such factors as poverty and economic depression were conducive for compulsive living.

Yet, my compulsiveness can help me to be free and spontaneous. Knowing that I am compulsive can motivate me to set structures that encourage me to enjoy and let go. In a paradoxical sense, I can compulsively allow myself to be free. Situations like recreation, solitude, and "doing nothing" *must* be constantly implemented. I must also be vigilant in claiming my compulsive tendencies. When a task is unfinished or done imperfectly, I can ask myself what difference it really makes. I can remind myself to let go. Using my compulsiveness creatively can help me to live a conscientious and disciplined life that leads to freedom and creativity.

CHAPTER SIX

Marginal Madness

Some people are not clearly normal or abnormal. Though they usually have some difficulty functioning in our normal formation, they are not sufficiently abnormal or disruptive to be hospitalized. For instance, neurotic people are usually accepted, but their behavior, unlike normal behavior, is seldom admired or striven for. As long as they are careful and not too troublesome, they can fit in with most of us and function rather normally. Others, like many alcoholics, may live precariously, and though they may be irritating, we usually tolerate them. Some marginal people, however, can become too embarrassing or troublesome and are put away until they act sufficiently normal. And if they cannot return to normalcy (like some old people), we can keep them permanently "out."

Unlike those of us who have our mad moments, marginally mad people are more inclined to live a mad life. But unlike normally mad life-styles and transactions, their madness is not socially rewarded and encouraged and is at best passively accepted. Although marginally mad people usually live in normal formation, "they" are not exactly one of "us"—not really full fledged members of the normal madness club. Rather, they hang on as "associate members" who may some day be fully accepted.

Unlike normal madness, the key dynamic of marginal (and abnormal) modes of madness is not the repression and/or forgetting of spirituality. Since the dynamics that constitute marginal (and abnormal) madness differ from those of normal madness, marginally mad persons are not quite normal, and yet they may live better and more meaningful lives than some normal people. For instance, neurotic persons, though fixated in certain areas, may grow in spirituality. They can live in and promote love and consequently may be more authentic and happier than normal people who forget the spirit of life. Of course, neurotic people can also lose their spirit and consequently compound their madness.

To reaffirm a radical distinction: Healthiness and holiness differ. Authentic healthiness (to grow in wholeness) includes holiness or spirituality, but holiness need not include healthiness. It is quite possible for people to be marginally or abnormally mad and live lives of love. A person can be a sick saint. Because of early childhood and perhaps constitutional factors, some people have little realistic chance of becoming healthy; nevertheless, they can live meaningful and significant lives. Though seldom consistently whole, they can be holy.

We will discuss how marginal madness can impede or help spirituality. The thesis is that marginal madness can indeed be an obstacle to and influence negatively our spiritual lives, and such madness can also challenge and strengthen our spirits. And though spirituality can cure normal madness, spirituality heals marginal and abnormal madness. In love marginally and abnormally mad people are less likely to identify with their problems and more likely to accept, integrate, and transcend them. When lived in the spirit, life takes on more meaning than merely normal satisfaction and success.

NEUROTIC MADNESS

Consider a neurotic person as one who is compelled to defend against significant experiences and who consequently feels condemned to repeat patterns of behavior that are contrary to healthy self-emergence. For example, the basis of neurosis may be repression, (perhaps of hostility and sexuality), that underlies compulsive behavior.

A dominant symptom of neurosis is anxiety evoked by unacceptable, senseless, or negative conflict. Neurotic anxiety means that I feel pressured to experience something new—to change, and simultaneously I feel I cannot and should not change—that I must maintain my identity. An example would be when I feel hostile and a counterforce not to be hostile. I have learned that the ultimate sin is to feel (not necessarily to act) hostile, and since I am hostile, I feel at odds with myself. I waste myself learning behavior that protects and maintains my neurotic identity: "I am not a hostile person." Ironically, the more I deny my true identity, the more hostile I can become; that is, my "no" to myself reinforces hostility toward myself and others. Ideally, I ought to listen to myself, make sense of my neurotic experience (I probably have reason to be hostile), and become—change—more of myself. The neurotic paradox is that I would rather live anxiously and precariously in being what I am not than admit to who I am and consequently live more easily and creatively.

But unlike most psychotic persons and like most normal persons, I can function in society. I do not seriously misinterpret social reality, nor do I manifest a high degree of personal disorganization; however, I am not completely normal and I move against healthy self-emergence. My existence becomes a futile and restless resistance against being open to certain experiences. While striving to be normal, I fight many unnecessary battles— and, the main enemy is myself. It is as if I find myself compelled to juggle many lead balls.

I pay a high price for being neurotic. I live with severe discomfort which can take various forms such as phobia, lethargy, compulsiveness, intense anxiety. And though I do not grossly misinterpret reality, I can feel condemned to set patterns of unhealthy behavior. And at times I may feel that I have lost control of my life or that life is almost intolerable. Along with having a very negative self-image, I can easily feel hurt and rejected.

But it makes sense to be neurotic. My madness serves to bind or control anxiety so I can live in normal formation. My primary "gain" is to conceal from myself unacceptable experiences—to maintain a false identity, which is why I often have the feeling of not being at home with myself. Secondary gains like attention, sympathy, and lack of responsibility can also be acquired. For example, I may become hyperdependent as a way of repressing and controlling unacceptable feelings of aggression and resentment and as a way of being liked and loved. I feel that if I did express all my feelings, I would be rejected or at least not be loved as much. My hyperdependent behavior is a compromise that enables me to control aggression and be loved. Much time and energy, however, is invested in trying not to be angry, and my dependency could impede autonomous and interdependent living.

Spiritual living is no cure for neurotic disorders, but spirituality can help people accept and transcend their neuroses. Instead of being suffocated by their madness, they can breathe more easily when they integrate their neuroses with their spirituality. Spirituality can give a neurotic existence more than discomfort and futile battles. It can give them integrity, dignity, and meaning that permanently permeates their lives. We will indicate in the following example how neurotic people, in spite of and because of their neuroses, can become holy people.

Some neurotic people try to repress unacceptable experiences, but their repression is so weak that they find themselves immersed in anxiety. Although such anxious people usually realize that their anxiety goes beyond a realistic fear, they are usually unaware of what makes them anxious, which is usually the repression of a significant experience. For instance, in anxious situations I may speak loudly or be over solicitous so that people may get tense and perhaps angry with me and too often miss my genuine care. Thus, I can temper my anxious behavior, and hopefully people will see through my anxiety to my love.

A more common type of anxiety neurosis occurs when a person gets very anxious when involved in certain situations. For instance, a man who is afraid of women may cope well with his own sex, but when confronted by women, he becomes uneasy and panicky. To withdraw from women to protect his unhealthy identity could easily militate against spiritual growth. But to face what he fears—women—would call for courage. Such a confrontation in love may not purge his fear but could help him to accept and transcend his fear—to fear in love.

Although neurotically depressed persons can function in normal society, they feel as if they have an extra burden to carry. They look at life too much with narrow and introspective eyes and often feel a persistent sense of guilt. Sometimes their deflated existence evokes sympathy but usually they become burdensome to others, and consequently have more reason to be depressed.

Depressed people may look for impending doom often because of unconscious ambivalence toward loved ones. They love and "hate" a person, and instead of admitting to their hostility, they repress it and punish themselves. Their life is precarious because they are afraid that their hostility may some day cancel their love. This possible loss can induce depression and their repressed anger can reinforce depression. The ideal is to admit to and learn from mixed feelings and consequently go beyond depression.

But depression does not and need not excuse me from loving. Even though I feel burdened, I can still move in love. Because of my depression, I may be extra sensitive to others' losses—especially in loneliness and death. And I may take extra precaution to foster experiences that are light and hopeful. Rather than exacerbating my depression, such experiences can save me from feeling totally lost.

I can present myself to God no matter how I feel. There need be no strings attached to my relationship with God—strings like being "happy," secure, not depressed. Even though I may feel vaguely guilty or unworthy, I can still reach out in love, for God will take me no matter how I am.

Unfortunately, we put too many conditions on our love relationships. We tend to say: "I love you in spite of your depression, hostility, guilt, and lethargy," implying that I would love you more if you were the way I want you to be. Such good intentions can easily make you feel more unworthy and depressed. The ideal is to love you unconditionally—no matter what. Then you are likely to be less depressed.

Depression can also help me to slow down to appreciate life more. Instead of controlling and using life, I may learn to respect and enjoy life. In my depression I may hear the poverty of spirit that proclaims being over having. And to be with in love is the paramount mode of being.

Obsessive compulsiveness is the neurotic style of people who want conditions one hundred percent right before acting. Perfect control makes them feel safe and especially when undergoing stress, they frantically try to make everything right. A scrupulous man, for example, may be attracted to a woman, yet feel sinful. To relieve his guilt and anxiety, he may compulsively try to say a set of prayers or perform a series or penitential acts perfectly. Perhaps after an hour or more of perfect penance, he feels all right.

When a situation does not run according to their plan, obsessive compulsive people can become extremely critical of themselves and others to make the situation conform to their views. They are willing to do almost anything as long as things turn out right, and when things are not perfect, they feel anxious and depressed and feel compelled to make things perfect. For instance, I can make others conform to my views, and when anyone or anything is out of line, I become critical and hostile. A comfortable and worthwhile life depends on everything being "just right" and everybody acting the way they "should." Such control protects me from threat—the spontaneous and unknown, and enables me to keep my neurotic identity: to be perfect.

Living out of their heads, compulsive people feel they have the possibility of making things all right. They may fantasize for days about a perfect encounter, or after an experience they may ruminate for hours to make things all right. They try to do the impossible: to make life perfect.

Consider the man who thinks for weeks about dating a woman, and after making the date, thinks for days about what might happen, what might go wrong, and what should happen. After the date, he is obsessed with what she might have thought of him, how it could and should have gone, and how imperfectly he acted. After hours or days of re-thinking and perhaps some compulsive penance for not being perfect, he feels some semblance of peace.

Obsessive compulsive persons cannot accept normal imperfections. Since they feel fully accepted only when they present the ideal to another, they find it painfully difficult to be their real, limited self. These persons have to learn to give up their ideal self and accept and be their real self with all its perfections and imperfections.

In a sense, obsessive compulsive people want to be God—to know everything, to have complete control, to be perfect. And especially when under stress, they will not settle for anything less than the kingdom of God on earth—they want everyone and everything to be perfect. Such a will to perfection can lead to a spiritual arrogance that conveys that "I am the way, the light and the truth."

My neurosis, however, can urge me to grow imperfectly in perfection. Realizing my perfectionistic style, I can be especially aware of accepting my imperfections. I can learn to affirm and even enjoy the loose ends and radical limitedness of being on earth. And because I tend to be proud, I can grow in humility—to come down to earth and celebrate my place on it.

Actually I can use my obsessiveness to be more open and spontaneous. I can be constantly aware of my particular demons—those that center around perfectionism. And I can structure my life in ways that allow and pressure me to let go. Play, celebration, leisure, and doing nothing can help me to transcend my neurosis. To promote spirituality in non-compulsive and yet constant ways can help me to be infinitely more than neurotic.

My obsessiveness can actually challenge me to grow in obedience and consequently become the author of my life. Because I can get locked into set patterns of behavior, I can be careful to listen to all sources of truth—God, myself, others, community, the law, tradition, etc. Because I know that I can be deafened by a cacophony of "shoulds," I listen more openly to experience and can see more alternatives for action. Instead of being obsessive, I can learn to be autonomous.

In love I may find the courage to be afraid rather than hiding from my fears. More basically: I can be both afraid and loved. I need not function perfectly to be loved. I need not listen openly to be heard. I need not see clearly to be seen. I need not move to be moved. I can love and be loved no matter how malfunctioning I am.

Another type of neurosis occurs when we can "convert" fears into such symptoms as blindness, deafness, and paralysis. Although our organs are physically healthy, they do not function. Usually such persons do not become totally incapacitated, but partially so. For instance, they learn selective deafness, only hearing what they want to hear and being deaf to threat.

Frigidity and impotence can be seen in a similar light. Although a frigid woman is anatomically sound, she becomes partially paralyzed and unable to give herself completely. The same is true for the impotent man: Although he may want to give himself, he fails in his attempts. Although consciously they usually want to give, neither of them can stand in the intimacy and vulnerability of sex. Their fear of being hurt or destroyed urges them to withdraw. Frigidity and impotence can make sense. For instance, a frigid woman's "no" to sexual fulfillment and to her partner may be a dignified stand if her partner is manipulative. Rather than playing normally mad games of love, she affirms that sex should include authentic love. Actually, her frigidity could be a demand for spirituality to be integrated with sexuality. The impotent man's "no" is often a part of a lifestyle that seeks a more solid stand, especially toward women. His genital impotence could be a sign that he wants to be more wholly present, that he wants to give himself spiritually as well as physically. Instead of only "performing well," he may really want to love and to be loved.

Some people dissociate parts of themselves. The most common instance occurs when I "cut out" part of my memory to protect myself from unacceptable experiences. Another kind of dissociative state, a fugue state, occurs when I function for a time and cannot recall (amnesia) what happened. The classic dissociative reaction is the multiple or split personality—the person who has two or more personality dimensions that function independently of one another.

My consistent and convenient forgetting can help me to be more thoughtful. Besides taking pains to remember, I can be sensitive to people's feelings. And though fugue states and multiple personalities are rare, they do occur and can include spiritual living. To maintain different lives within the same person, however, is exhausting and can consequently impede a person's spiritual life. The ideal is to integrate myself so I can present my whole being to God and others. But if this does not happen, God still takes me as I am. Unfortunately, people seldom do the same.

Many of us experience phobias—inappropriate and anxious fears toward situations. Frequently, phobias are nuisances that we manage, but when they overwhelm and control our life, we can become neurotic. For example, we can experience mild episodes of claustrophobia (feeling anxious in closed-in places) and tolerate it or take precaution that it is unlikely to occur. But we become neurotic when controlled or incapacitated by claustrophobia. When we are unable to work because we cannot ride in cars and elevators or function in an office, we are probably neurotic.

I can be phobic in almost all areas, including love. If I am a phobic lover, I am overwhelmed with an intense fear of intimacy:

When faced with the opportunity to love, I panic and feel weak. One possibility is that my love phobia may be a defense against forbidden desires and drives, like intimacy. Love is consciously feared but unconsciously wanted, and perhaps forbidden. "Philophobia" could be learned through traumatic or consistently painful experiences. If I am brutally rejected in love, I can fear love. Or consider the child who is made fun of, left alone, or sees the parents playing marital games. It is not surprising that this person is leery of, or fears that foreign experience called love.

Such philophobia can have deleterious effects on my spiritual life. Being afraid to love, I may play "safe" and withdraw from situations where love may be likely to occur. Although within my spirit I may crave love, I am also scared to death of it. Thus, I abstain from the food I need most and consequently starve. The essence of spirituality—love—is defended against or fought off as if it were an enemy instead of a saving grace.

I must be willing to be afraid in love and perhaps risk dying in love. But which is better: To die in love or to live without love? I can discover that I stand on common ground with everyone else, that all of us can find it more or less risky to love. But when I take the leap in love, I may find my spirit come alive. Even though I may get hurt, my pain is an affirmation of my love —the heart of the matter.

Still another way of being neurotic is to fight life so much that I constantly feel weak, tired, and sometimes exhausted. I use considerable energy to repress myself and consequently have less energy to promote life. I usually sleep too much, lack enthusiasm for anything, and chronically complain. I ride the neurotic merry-go-round—the more anxious I become, the more I repress, and the more I repress the more anxious I become.

One of my challenges is to stop and be—and be who I am: tired, weak, restless. I can present myself as I am rather than fighting myself. I can realize that in love I can be embraced no matter how I feel. And paradoxically in love I can come to feel more alive, stronger, and serene. My life need not simply be a series of neurotic battles, but I can rest at times in love.

People, however, can manifest similar symptoms when in a critical period of growth. For instances, persons in critical periods of growth (an adolescent, young adult, adult, middle ager, or an elderly person) can be tired and irritable because of the struggle to find and be themselves. This tiredness is often in service of growth, whereas neurotic fatigue is the price of stagnation. Spiritual crises can also incorporate times of fatigue that could be invalidly interpreted as negative or bad. For example, I may find that I need more sleep or that I want to work less. Spiritual emergence is always embodied and therefore affects concrete living.

Neurotic difficulty may also be seen in a preoccupation with health. A hypochondriacal stance may enable me to get sympathy and attention and may basically divert attention from my low self-esteem and feelings of unworthiness. Usually, you may initially feel sorry for me, but the more you know me, the more you withdraw. My constant complaints become irritating, intrusive, and exploitive. For various reasons, I feel unaccepted unless I am sick.

A danger is to play the martyr role. I feel worthy only as a sick person who needs to be cured. I fail to realize that I am always in need of being healed—of becoming more whole in and through love. I can hide my true vulnerability and incompleteness behind sickness. I must try to be a true martyr—to give in love for the sake of love.

An important point is that, if we are neurotic, often we have learned to become neurotic in childhood. By the time we have reached the age of authentic freedom, in adolescence or young adulthood, we have usually been conditioned to live neurotically. For example, the hypochondriacal lover may have learned in childhood that the best way to feel accepted, affirmed, and loved is to feel sick or "not good."

Neurotic persons, however, are not necessarily programmed

for life. When young, we can usually only see those possibilities that are given to us, but as we get older, we can discover different alternatives. For instance, I can see my parents differently by accepting and understanding (not necessarily condoning) them. Perhaps I cannot and should not forget, but I can learn to forgive. Even though they may initially and sometimes always reject my love, I can always offer it. I can understand and transcend their fears and my own, in and through love. I can discover that I do not automatically have to respond in fixed ways, but can change my behavior to help both myself and others. By experiencing new meaning in past and present behavior, I can change in the future.

Fortunately, my life does not depend on being healthy—on not being neurotic. My life depends on love. Health is not available to everyone, but spirituality is. We need not be healthy to live a life of love. Love incorporates all of us no matter who or what we are. Love is our saving grace. Consequently, healthiness is the ideal to be striven for, but spirituality is the way that is available to all and that is necessary for permanently positive meaning.

We can also ask how we (normals) can help them (neurotics). We must begin with ourselves, by claiming our own madness and discerning whether our madness evokes and promotes their madness. Also we can appreciate that we and they are much more similar than different. We must be careful not to pull rank on or patronize them—"the neurotic nuts"—in order to hide our own madness. Our only hope is based on the fact that we are one of a kind.

It might shake us out of our normal arrogance to realize that we are not superior to those who are not normal. In fact, it might be sobering to realize that neurotic persons can be better people than we are. Neurotic persons can have a sensitivity and depth that we lack. We might even try to act superior because they intimidate us—they evoke our own uncertainty and indict our spiritual paucity.

PSYCHOSOMATIC DISORDERS

A psychosomatic disorder is a physical disorder, like a head-ache, ulcer, or high blood pressure, presumably caused by emotional or psychological factors. Most researchers agree that a constant and unacceptable amount of emotional stress can cause psychosomatic illness and that people may be unaware of their emotional state. For instance, though obvious to others, I may be a compulsive workaholic who is not consciously aware that I live a pressured life, worry about almost everything, and seldom recreate. If I get an ulcer, I seem surprised and fail to re-evaluate and change my style of living. Furthermore, some scientists think that persons can inherit a predisposition toward a certain type of psychosomatic illness or that persons will manifest their disorder in a weak or significant part of their bodies. For instance, one workaholic may get a stomach ulcer, while another under similar stress has migraine headaches.

Psychosomatic disorders are so common that some physicians think that many complaints of patients are psychosomatic. Furthermore, an ulcer or heart attack can be seen facetiously as a sign of success: If you do not suffer from one before you are thirty-five, you are probably not trying hard enough. Our concern is the relationship between psychosomatic illness and normal madness.

Psychosomatic illness can be an abnormal sign of our normal madness. When I am not living as fully as I can or am missing too much of life, my body may protest. My bodily disorder may indicate that my pace and place are too normal and mad. Consider a mother of six children with migraine headaches. She may be experiencing constant stress not only because of her children but also because of her boring routines, a phantom husband and father, poor marital relations, minimal self-esteem, hyperdependency, lack of recreation, and in general her too normal way of living. Day in and day out her life gets tighter and more insipid instead of freer and more alive. She finds herself going deeper into a spiritless life. Her stressful and boring life may call for headaches—a symptom that may be better treated with more autonomy, serenity, and spiritual meaning rather than with pills.

Our stress can come primarily from inside or outside ourselves, or both. If I am a workaholic who must make every minute count, I can pay the price of psychosomatic illness. My compulsion to cope with life as if it were only a task can easily put me on edge and exhaust me. Coupled with my dependency on work, my inability to do nothing, to play, and to enjoy the mystery of living, results in my being a fragmented, incomplete, and tense person whose madness may be manifested in high blood pressure or a heart attack. Or if my job is boring, I can feel locked in a meaningless situation. Spending much of my time senselessly can cause tension that may even increase under the demands of a family. My daily routine can evoke and promote daily stress that causes an ulcer. Or if I am a compulsive teacher of high school sophomores, I am an excellent candidate for a psychosomatic disorder. When I try to maintain complete order, I am fighting a losing battle. In failing to accept and to appreciate the healthy disorder of these early adolescents, I become disordered while trying to hide behind a mask of perfection. Since I fruitlessly use my functional authenity in lieu of personal authenity, the students encounter a role instead of a person, and consequently they are even more disruptive. I may find myself left with not much more than one big headache.

Although persons with a psychosomatic illness can often be helped with medication, a danger is to escape with medication instead of being responsible for the illness. We can spend much time and money learning to depend on drugs instead of depending on ourselves. Or instead of changing our lives, we may change our body by having parts of it surgically removed. We see our disorder only as a physical illness that we have and that can be removed surgically, not also as a disorder we are and can learn from. We ought to listen to our discomfort to discover what it may be saying about our lives. Perhaps our bodies are bearing the pain of spiritual emptiness. Perhaps in a very embodied way we are protesting for spiritual life.

Thus, psychological stress and its psychosomatic concommitants can be the result of and an indictment of normal madness. An ulcer or hypertension may be saying: "Listen to me! I am protesting your life. Take stock of your life. How are you living? Look at what you are uptight about. Are you missing much of life? Stop living this way and change your life! Live more freely and fully. Where is your spirit?"

DRUG ADDICTION

Consider drug addicts as persons who must take drugs to function normally. Without drugs, they become so upset, physiologically and psychologically, that they fail to cope with ordinary demands. Addicts see drugs as their ultimate concern—drugs are their paramount source of satisfaction, and without them they feel painfully inadequate and meaningless. The compulsion to take drugs is mad, but society often accepts and sometimes approves this behavior.

When addicted, we lack autonomy though we may strive for perfection. Whether or not professionally successful, we feel like failures who have not realized our ideals. On drugs, there are no worries or cares—everything and everybody are leveled. When we de-orbit from our euphoria, however, we may feel even more inadequate and perhaps guilty. Consequently, there may be a greater need to go on another trip.

Since alcoholism is the most frequent and quasi-normal type of drug addiction, we focus on it more than other types of addiction. Although there is a strong movement to make alcoholism a disease, many people do not entirely accept this diagnosis. To see alcoholism as an illness like a broken arm or the flu often does not make much sense to many normal people and to alcoholics. Still, alcoholism can be likened to a disease insofar as a person cannot rationally choose to stop being an alcoholic, but alcoholism is also a way of living—a style that a person is—not only a disease that a person has.

Alcoholism is usually on the borderline of normality and abnormality. It is a form of drug addiction that is usually tolerated, often accepted, and frequently supported. When alcoholics intrude too much on our lives, they are ostracized though usually not in an institution; the ostracism is more subtle. For example, if I am "the family alcoholic," I am usually tolerated and minimally recognized as a person. But my family may unknowingly pressure me to drink because "they" need "me" to drink. They may look down on me to gain a false sense of superiority and healthiness. Or they might use me as a scapegoat and displace their anger on me while playing martyr roles. Too often an alcoholic is subtly supported, but seldom is an alcoholic seen as a possible result of social (including family) processes.

Alcoholics often have high hopes and ideals that they feel they have never fulfilled. For example, although I may be very successful in business, I may have wanted to be an artist, but somehow went along with the normal flow of life and settled for satisfaction and success. One of the reasons I am an alcoholic may be because I did not have the courage or support to pursue my spiritual values. To a degree, alcoholism can be the price one pays for being too normal.

Paradoxically, alcoholism can be a mad attempt to cope with the madness of normality. Alcohol can serve to numb my painful feelings, like loneliness and emptiness, that indict conventional madness. Alcohol can give me a temporary feeling of contentment and sometimes the illusion of power. Stumbling out of normal formation, I can feel out of this world. I need not and cannot be concerned and cope with what is going on around and within me. My spiritual frustration is ameliorated and my spiritual growth is frustrated. Alcohol numbs my pain, protects me, and turns me in on myself. I can withdraw into my chemical closet and float away.

Alcohol abuse can also be an abnormal way of being normal. Under the influence of alcohol, I may be given special license that I normally do not have. I may act a bit "mad" and blame it on the alcohol. For instance, I can cry my blues, criticize everyday madness, or perhaps dance with abandon. A rule, however, is that I can only act within certain limits, and if I persistently embarrass, impede, or hurt others, I am ostracized, and possibly institutionalized.

Street corner addicts, however, not only try to escape from themselves but also frequently from society's inequities that may pressure them to be marginal people. And to support a heroin addiction, which can cost $100.00 per day, addicts may steal, sell themselves, push dope, or hustle in various ingenious ways. Both society (we) and individual addicts (they) are exploited and violated. Addicts do offend society, and they should take the responsibility to change their lives. Still, our pressure of normal madness can be a significant dynamic of addiction, but we seldom admit to our guilt and responsibility. We (legal normals) would rather blame or feel sorry for them (illegal addicts). Rather than reconciling ourselves, we foster a fragmented society.

Taking normal drugs can be a mode of madness that is more subtle than first appears. On one hand, a heroin addict is usually considered more abnormal than normal unless he or she is wealthy enough to afford a steady supply of drugs. On the other hand, many normal people, though not illegal addicts are legal ones. We can be addicted to or dependent on barbiturates, stimulants, anti-depressants, or tranquilizers. Drugs give us relief from pain and help us to function normally. Since we become normal via drugs, most people accept and often encourage us.

We normals often take drugs to quiet feelings like boredom, depression, and loneliness that indict our spiritual emptiness. Instead of listening to our feelings, we can try to kill them and thereby violate ourselves. Our existence is tenuous and precarious, chemical and artificial. Being too dependent on factors outside ourselves, we lack the autonomy and integrity that are essential for a mature and healthy life.

Still, we normal addicts can become incensed when we see our children taking so-called street drugs. We may have little awareness that children may have been raised in a subtle but real drug culture. Children can see and emulate our taking drugs (including alcohol) to maintain ourselves and to escape spiritual pain. Although we may feel that our children are totally different from us, they may be following our normal and mad lives.

A seductive force of drugs is that some can activate our forgotten spirit. Certain drugs can liberate us from our mental sets and categorical approach to life and thereby enable us to experience more than what is normal. On drugs, we can see differently and some of these visions may include the spiritual. A difficulty is that such a spiritual liberation, which does not always occur, happens at the pace of the drug rather than at our particular pace. Depending on the drug and minimizing our autonomy, we will probably find it very difficult or impossible to integrate our spiritual insights. We can become more frustrated and hopeless.

Whether we are on drugs to free or to shackle our spirits, our hope is that we are spiritual beings. We can listen to what we are numbing, to what is contained. The spirit of an alcoholic may be drenched in alcohol and yet be crying loudly for love. The spirit of a junkie may be broken but nevertheless there to be embraced. Our spirits can be broken, numbed, contained, lost, hurt, but never completely destroyed.

SEX OFFENDERS

Many people see sex offenders as the most detested of persons. Many of us view the sex offender as the dirty old idiot who lurks in the shadows waiting for the virgin whom he rapes viciously. Actually, sex offenders (with the exception of most rapists) are usually not vicious but are often passive, sensitive, and intelligent. Unlike neurotic persons, they may not experience anxiety or lead a hyperdefensive life, and unlike psychotic persons, they may not experience ego disintegration, withdrawal from reality, or severe mood swings. Sex offenders usually function normally and appear to be as normal as us, but when under stress, they feel pressured to act out sexually. Instead of alcohol or other drugs, being neurotic or psychotic, or playing normal games, they find relief and meaning in a sex offense. Though sex offenders usually function normally, we usually consider that their sexual behavior is so disgusting that we put them in jail and sometimes in a hospital. "They are certainly not one of us," so we say.

We have seen that we can also offend against sex but not in socially offensive ways. When we use sex to gain self-satisfaction and power, we are mad. Sex merely to relieve tension, to produce children, or to escape from loneliness is normal and mad. Sex without genuine care is mad. Both normal and abnormal sex offenders violate people. Abnormal sex offenders, however, are often more destructive than normal ones; nevertheless, "they" are not the only sex offenders. "We" can too easily use "them" as scapegoats to give ourselves the illusion of innocence or of healthy sex. The fact is that much of our sex is mad—without spirit.

Indeed, sex offenders are mad: They exploit people, repress experiences, and satisfy themselves in unhealthy ways. They should be made to make restitution and they should be helped. But we too can be sex offenders—normal rather than abnormal ones. When we exploit, repress, or seek satisfaction without love, we are mad and should make restitution and be helped. The basis of creative restitution and growth is love.

MENTALLY DEFICIENT PERSONS

We can think of mentally retarded persons as people who function sub-normally in the intellectual realm. In growing up, they have more than average difficulty in learning and sometimes in social adjustment and personal maturity. Some mentally retarded persons can lead autonomous lives, most have some difficulty, and others are totally dependent. The intention is not to go through the various dynamics and degrees of mental retardation, but to look at mentally deficient persons in light of our approach.

Some mentally retarded people can be taught to take care of themselves and to hold a job—to be normal. Instead of putting them in institutions as in the past, we can be taught to teach them to become productive members of society. And there are places where mentally retarded people live in non-institutional settings where they work as well as and can be happier than many of us.

Nevertheless, mentally retarded persons are more or less abnormal in light of many normal standards. Although they can often maintain themselves, they probably have difficulty in competitive situations—especially those that call for efficiency and lead to success. Their adjustment to many normal situations is below (normal) par, though they are usually tolerated, patronized, or minimized. They clearly fall short of our cultural values like rationality, information, having, and equality. Although mentally deficient persons can be healthy "abnormal" persons who live in a normally mad world, sometimes they are genuinely accepted, other times passively tolerated, and too often rejected. Instead of respecting them, we may pity and patronize them. Some of us can only feel intelligent and competent in reference to mentally deficient people. We can try to gain a false sense of superiority by making them inferior.

Actually, mentally retarded persons are our equals, for they are one of us—humans. And they may be superior to us, for rational knowledge is not necessary to experience transrational love. Though intelligence is one of many factors that can make a difference—positive or negative, higher intelligence does not necessarily improve love. Or conversely, low intelligence does not necessarily impede or lessen love. The fact is that a mentally retarded person can be a better lover and therefore a better person, than a genius.

Nevertheless, we reward geniuses and ostracize the retarded. Perhaps retarded persons with their simple presence indict our intellectual and technocratic madness and our paucity of spirituality. Perhaps these "dummies" point out our lack of wisdom. Perhaps these "retardos" indict our stunted lives of love.

Mentally retarded persons may seem cheated, yet their lack of intelligence could have merit. Lacking a certain rational sophistication, they might seem primitive and unhealthy, but actually they can have a certain simplicity, transparency, and depth. A lack of intelligence also makes it more difficult to play normal games, especially of thinking too much and of manipulating others. Life is inclined to be pure and direct and less likely to be normally mad. For example, if I am a mentally retarded person, I may be less apt to analyze, categorize, or take life for granted. More likely my life is a life filled with exploration and surprise, especially with concrete and simple realities. I may have genuine fun with things, show delight in activities, really enjoy nature, be warmly close to animals, and be honest and true with people. This "dumb" person may live with more depth and integrity than most of us.

Although mentally retarded persons may seem to be childlike, lacking pretense and gamesmanship, they are not the same as normal children. Their feelings are more developed and their wealth of experiences are greater than a child's. An equal mistake is to treat them as though they were normal adults. They do not think or always behave the same as us. Mentally retarded persons are somewhere between childhood and adulthood and yet they are not adolescent. We should respect and appreciate them for who they are—persons, the same as us.

BRAIN DAMAGED PERSONS

One of the most abused and forgotten of the marginal people are brain damaged persons. They are usually elderly persons who have lived a normal life and who find themselves losing normal functions that they took for granted. To various degrees they lose their rational functions—a key sign of abnormality. Recent recall is impaired; abstract thinking and comprehension are usually subnormal; new learning is often difficult; judgment may be clouded; speech may thicken; visual-motor coordination is often clumsy. Severe damage can cause disorientation. Brain damaged persons can also manifest psychotic behavior, though not always, and in the most severe instances, they become childish and incapacitated.

Since the brain damaged persons are often seen as burdensome, hopeless, or somewhat less than human, they are often ostracized or contained. Researchers and clinicians have found, however, that persons with brain damage are often capable of doing more than we might think. Sometimes they can be retrained to function normally or at least taught to meet the minimum demands of life. Still, it is not rare to see normal people institutionalize their parents at or away from home because they get in their way and are troublesome. Is abnormal functioning a just reason to be placed and forgotten in a junkyard for old people?

Brain damaged persons' lack of some rational functions does not mean that they lack a capacity to receive and give. They may be capable of living more deeply than normal people with good memories and sharp intelligence. So what if they do repeat the same story? The process of sharing and reliving history are far more important than conveying information. Still, we see elderly people as useless—people who can no longer produce, compete, be successful, adjust, be powerful—be normal. Like children, the elderly only have themselves to offer.

Regardless of brain damage, just being old is considered an abnormality that many of us tolerate at best. Old people (especially with brain damage) are seldom seen in normal formation, but are more likely to be hidden and controlled. And we often pressure elderly people to play the game of being old: be withdrawn, silent, dependent, docile, dumb, worthless, and allow others to be mad. To act otherwise would threaten too many normals. Old age in itself is a threat—it is so close to death that it summons us to take stock of our lives. Consequently, we seldom respect and listen to old people.

We may be afraid to admit that "they" intimidate "us." Being close to death, they can indict our mad lives. Dying summons us to live—to rekindle our impoverished spirits. But the normal and mad way is to deny death and to silence its message: Live. Death exposes our madness and calls for more authentic and permanent living. Without the spirit of life—love, death, becomes an absurd annihilation. We do try to help them medically, economically, and socially and certainly this assistance is often necessary and good. But the possible madness is that we manipulate the elderly to silence their indictments. Why can we not embrace them and invite them to be with us? Why do they have to be categorized as "them" instead of being one together? Old people desire more than normal treatment and caretaking, and they deserve personal interest, appreciation, respect, delight, and love.

CHAPTER SEVEN

Abnormal Madness

"Sure, I'd like to get better, to be healthy—whatever that means. Do you think I like having experiences against my will—especially the voices that tell me I'm impure and no good. Do you think it's fun to feel panicky—that you'll fall apart in front of everyone and be called crazy and taken to a hospital? Then you see the doctor who tells you what's wrong with you. The M.D.—you know: mostly divine, or is it mentally deficient—recommends shock, drugs, or brutal speech therapy. How do you think I feel? How would you like working part time in programs tailored for you—a metally ill patient. I'd die to be able to have a normal job.

"I know I spend more time in fantasy than reality. I know my love for priests goes overboard, that I spend too much time in thinking what it would be like for a priest to hold and love me. I know it's crazy when I hear them talk to me—but, for God's sake, if I give up my fantasies and priests, what do I have left? Nothing! At least my fantasies are mine; they give me more than anything else. And yet the therapeutic plumbers keep telling me to give up my fantasies and to replace them with reality. What reality? Can you tell me where to find it? Tell me, how can I find what my fantasies offer, what the voices tell me, and be normal?"

This 20-year-old woman is angry about how she was and can be treated. Paradoxically she speaks of the pain and pride, the absurdity and meaning of her life. Like many abnormally disordered people, she does not realize her potential to the fullest possible extent. The lives of abnormally mad persons are closed, defensive, and fixated, and are often fraught with confusion, anxiety, and loss. These psychotic people lose normal contact with normal reality so that they have extreme difficulty in meeting the everyday demands of living. They suffer notable mood alterations, and they can experience severe distortion of thought and perception. Unlike the neurotic persons, psychotic persons manifest much more psychic and functional disorganization. Psychotic persons, however, seldom want to be unhealthy but feel helplessly tied in psychological chains. Still, these mad people can manifest a certain sense in their madness and can witness to a strange dignity.

Abnormally mad persons differ from us in many ways. We normals basically satisfy needs, whereas they may have needs such as security and love which are unsatisfied. We adjust and accommodate to reality without serious fixation, incapacity, or disintegration and consequently cope moderately well in competitive and personal situations. Psychotic persons, however, are usually hurt by and afraid of these situations and withdraw from, are overwhelmed by, or are highly anxious in them. For whatever reason, abnormally mad persons cannot function normally: be satisfied, adjust or act efficiently. They are out of normal formation or painfully in it, and they often lack the power to change the situation.

Various kinds and degrees of abnormal madness exist. Some people are unhealthy as a fundamental way of life. Pathological processes permeate and influence almost anything they do. Being chronically shackled, they live their entire lives more or less in madness. Others manifest unhealthiness when in certain situations or when under stress. These people can usually function more or less normally, but when the stress (external or internal) becomes too great to handle, they fall apart. For example, I may be able to function well as long as I am supported and affirmed at work and by my family, but if I should lose my job and be rejected, I may become so depressed that I am incapacitated. Similarly, others have mad tendencies that are realized infrequently but are latently present. As long as these people are in a safe and stable environment, they function, but when confronted with serious stress, they behave abnormally.

Unlike normal madness, abnormal madness is often considered absurd. We (normals) see little or no sense in abnormal madness and consider it undesirable and possibly destructive. Abnormal madness is judged to be negative, meaningless, and no good. To think of it as possibly positive, meaningful, and good could seem mad. Yet we do not consider our normal madness in the same way. Unlike abnormal madness, we do not judge ourselves as absurd or as impeding or destroying integral living. "We" are not confined, treated, and controlled; "they" are. Instead of admitting to our own absurdities, we focus on their madness. Perhaps we and they are more similar than different. Perhaps we can learn from them.

ABNORMALLY MAD PEOPLE

Presently, abnormally mad people usually are called psychotic. Being out of normal formation, they have an existence that differs from ours. They find it difficult to meet the ordinary demands of life like holding a job and coping with everyday stress. Since they frequently cause an excessive amount of stress for themselves and others, they often disrupt normal functioning. Hallucinations and delusions may also be a part of their world and contribute to their confusion and incapacity to act normally.

We normal people can be so threatened by, confused with, or busy handling abnormal behavior that we are blind to the sense of the psychotic world. We usually see psychotics as poor and sick people who do not measure up to normal living. We think that until they get on the right track (our's), they are really not capable of meaningful experiences. When translated, statements such as "Come to your senses," "You're out of your mind," and "You're off your rocker and unreasonable," may mean "See reality as I see it," "You're not in my mind," and "Your style is not normal and you will not give up your convictions." The contention, however, is that psychotic persons can make as much sense as normal persons.

Being out of formation, psychotic people can be conspicuous and a cause for alarm. Regardless of the explanation for abnormal madness (mythical, religious, political, medical, psychological, sociological), we are wary of and may control, punish, or treat them. Somehow, they must be made normal—sensible, proper, constructive, predictable, comprehensible, and familiar—like us.

Psychotic persons are unhealthy, but they do not necessarily have a disease like polio, strep throat, or syphilis that must be diagnosed, treated, and gotten rid of. Rather than just "having" a disease, they "are" in the world in an abnormal way that makes both sense and non-sense. Unfortunately, being "psychotic" means that a person is judged incapable of making significant sense and of having important experiences. One need only read books like *The Inner World of Mental Illness* and *I Never Promised You a Rose Garden* to realize that psychotic people do speak significant sense. Or even better, try honestly loving and truthfully living with (not diagnosing, treating, and managing) psychotic people.

As long as psychotics keep weird experiences to themselves and behave within normal limits, we usually do not mind. When they let us know that they hear voices, we look at them with caution and label them as crazy. We seldom show compassion or try to understand the meaning of their painful experience, but instead focus on their behavior and judge it as meaningless and perhaps disruptive. When psychotic persons persist in sharing their voices and even speak differently than us, most of us become disturbed. And the more they unsettle our lives, the more likely they are to be put away. Psychotic people are often institutionalized and treated because mainly they disrupt and break down in the areas of rational thought, proper feelings, normal adjustment, and common sense.

The psychotic breakdown of normal functions, however,

could lead to a spiritual breakthrough. When hypernormality is rejected or dissipated, spirituality may emerge. Since normal madness may impede or prevent consistent spiritual experiences, the lack of normal madness in the form of abnormal madness could include spirituality. One reason is that mad processes such as thinking and feeling in set categorical ways that preclude spiritual emergence are sufficiently weakened and damaged to allow and even evoke spiritual emergence. For instance, if my hyper-rational approach to life dissipates, my transrational experiences are more likely to emerge.

To be sure: Psychotic breakdowns are not recommended for spiritual breakthroughs. There are easier, clearer, more direct and positive ways of rekindling latent spirituality. More importantly, psychotic spiritual emergence is a process that occurs beyond my freedom. Furthermore, the experience is more or less primitively symbolic and peculiar, and the lack of rational powers make it difficult to communicate, integrate, and implement. Nevertheless, when psychotic persons regain their rational processes, they can begin to foster spirituality in a healthy way.

Thus, a psychotic breakdown may mean that a person can no longer stand normal madness—the forgetting of spirituality, and the escape into abnormal madness can be an attempt to live a more authentic life, including spirituality. Psychotic persons may rather be unhealthy and authentic than normal and phony. The intense personal experiences of psychosis, though irrational and unhealthy, can include transrational experiences that can lead to healthier and happier living.

Consider this 28-year-old man. "You might say I was one of the craziest. I heard special messages over the radio and sometimes I even saw a news man telling me to save the world. I kind of knew this was crazy, but it made sense and seemed better than anything else. But I also had times when I felt I was going to be strangled by a kaleidoscope of nerve endings. I never want to go through it again. That's for sure. Yet I did learn some things, not that this is the best way to learn. Maybe it was necessary; I don't know. I do know that I am a better person—more sensitive, and I think, more solid inside. Strange to say, I think I'm a better person than before my breakdown.

"One of the biggest differences is that I'm really sensitive to the way people feel, especially how they can be hurt. I can really see through the games we play and how we hurt one another. In fact, I can simply see more of everything. It seems that before my breakdown, I was mainly trying to maintain things or to get a little bit ahead. It was like I was fighting life. Now I enjoy life. Instead of struggling all the time, I can really say that I love life."

Or think of this 52-year-old woman. "My family said I had a breakdown and the doctor said I had an involutional psychosis. Whatever, I never thought I could be so depressed and feel so useless. Life simply didn't make any sense, and I had no energy to do anything about it. I felt embarrassed and guilty—like I was letting my family down, but it seemed the more I tried, the worse things got. Our family doctor sent me to a specialist, and he gave me drugs. Although I felt a bit numb, life was no better; in fact, I think things got worse. Then I really felt crazy when the doctor recommended electric shock treatment. But the doctor said that only about six treatments would probably be necessary and that I need not be afraid. Believe me shock is no picnic. My memory is still fuzzy at times. Anyhow, I felt less depressed after "the" shock but still didn't feel like moving. And I soon became depressed again. After two more series of shock, the doctor mentioned probable long term hospitalization. I was ready to kill myself.

"Thank God, with the help of a different doctor I started to make sense of things. For instance, I found I had good reason to be depressed—like my kids did leave home to go to school and get married. Like I never really prepared for the changes in my life. Like nothing made sense. I really started to take stock of my life, and I'm glad to say that my husband and I are much closer now, and I'm glad to say, wiser. I'm not inclined to take life for granted. Listen, I'm not getting any younger; so, I'm going to live life to its fullest. Maybe my breakdown was a blessing, but those kinds of blessings I don't need. Still, I went down to hell, and though I'm not in heaven, I feel better than ever."

Think of schizophrenic persons, the most frequently diagnosed psychotics. They try to withdraw from our normal world into their own (abnormal) worlds. Their ability to think rationally is impaired, delusions and hallucinations may plague them, and their behavior is ambivalent and inappropriate as judged by an objective observer. For instance, some schizophrenic persons may seem to be simple and harmless, manifesting apathy and indifference. Though they seem to be dolts, they are really not. Unlike us, they seldom take the initiative of being actively and overtly involved. They do not bother anyone, and they want no one to bother them. Usually these kinds of people are left alone unless they are abnormally disruptive such as publically wearing too many clothes or constantly walking away when spoken to. Although their presence seems bland and flat, it is a mistake to think that they are incapable of meaningful experiences. Their preference for solitude, nature, or animals over people does not preclude a spiritual life. Their withdrawal from competitive and communal activities does not necessarily indicate a loveless life. If we enter into their world, we can discover that these disinterested persons can be interesting.

Other schizophrenics may withdraw into a catatonic state, usually in an apparent stupor. Although they appear lifeless and seem to be "out of it," they are attentive behind their dead facades to what is going on. These persons may want to extend themselves but feel it is too painful because they may have been vitally hurt. They might feel that if their bodies are made lifeless, they can no longer be hurt. They make their body a corpse to protect their spirit.

Consider a seventeen-year-old girl who was raped psychologically by her parents and physically by a sex offender. Her pain was so overwhelming and senseless that she wanted to die without killing herself. She found herself radically withdrawn from our normal world and from people who hurt her so much. As she described her experiences: "It was as if my body were 'a body' or 'somebody,' not my body. When they touched me, I could see what they were doing, but it didn't feel like it. It was like it wasn't me. I knew what was happening, but it was like it was happening to somebody else."

The most regressed schizophrenic, hebephrenic persons, can also have significant experiences. Their childish mannerisms, inappropriate giggling, regressive behavior, and disorganized thinking does not preclude spiritual experience. For example, a forty-year-old woman would work in the hospital laundry, but every two hours she would take time to feed her baby doll. When asked what she was doing, she said, as if she were a five-year-old, that she had to feed her baby. When told of her father's death, she said it was funny and laughed hysterically. Later, when alone, she sobbed. Though this woman is poignantly sick, she may give more love to her baby doll than many normals do to anyone. Though her spirit may be disguised with hebephrenic spirit, it nevertheless is expressed. To respect her spirit may make it less likely for her to hide.

Even the schizophrenics who manifest delusions of grandeur and/or persecution and who are hostile and suspicious are capable of spiritual experiences. Paranoid people are deathly afraid of people and consequently make people afraid of them. Their hateful eyes are actually ways of defending against others. For example, a twenty-seven-year-old man built a delusional world where he was the chief agent and innovator of a secret service that combated communism. He became extremely suspicious of people because they might be communists, and he constructed fantastically intricate plans of how to combat the enemy while constantly being careful that "they" would not discover him. His delusional world not only protected him but also gave him a feeling of worth; being safely persecuted may have felt better than being anxiously nothing. Though caught in a paranoid maze, his spirit still spoke.

No one knows for sure what causes people to be schizophrenic.

Some think that organic factors are the exclusive or main cause, and just as many or more researchers propose that childhood and especially family experiences evoke schizophrenic withdrawal. Still others try to integrate such organic and environmental approaches. It has not been our intention to discuss various etiologies of schizophrenia but to make sense of the apparent nonsense of schizophrenic and other modes of madness. When we really listen to schizophrenic people, we may find persons who are struggling to become intimate, but like most psychotics and many of us, they are afraid of the very thing they want. They want to live fully, but are afraid. They want to love, but are afraid that love will destroy them. When we show unconditional trust, compassionate patience, and honest presence, schizophrenic persons can begin to extend themselves to us.

Other psychotic persons may show bizarre behavior primarily in severe mood swings. For instance, people can become so depressed that they feel worthless and incapacitated. Some researchers think that psychotic depression is totally or partially caused by chemical or physiological processes, and others think that the main reasons are rooted in psychosocial and intrapsychic processes. Whatever the cause, depression is a mode of being in the world or an experience to understand and learn from, not just a disease that one has and must expunge.

Psychotically depressed persons frequently feel unworthy of love—"Who would love such an angry and worthless person?" They can repress forbidden feelings, like anger and hate, and pay the price of guilt, shame, and self-punishment. They may feel intense guilt for hating others whom they love or from whom they want approval, or they might feel violent anger that they repress and turn on themselves. In both situations, these depressed persons feel unable to admit to their feelings and still get love and approval. A depressed man, for example, might feel intense resentment toward his mother, but feels that if he admits his resentment, he would lose her affection. This person may constantly go out of his way to please his mother who may use and disapprove of him. A depressed person wants to be free but often feels compelled to hide anger. We must learn to listen to the sense of depression—that authentic care embraces all of a person, including ambivalence.

Psychotic people may also express the apparent opposite of depression: manic behavior. Even though they manifest elation, irritability, talkativeness, flight of ideas, and in general a highly accelerated pace, spirituality is not necessarily repressed, forgotten, or somehow cancelled. Think of this thirty-eight-year-old woman. One day, to the dismay of her family, she began to clean frantically and ceaselessly the entire house including ceilings, walls, and floors. Seemingly with boundless energy, she went on a buying spree which put her and her family in $8000.00 debt, and then she proceeded to dig her garden in the middle of winter. When asked what she was doing, she laughed sarcastically and accused her family of not appreciating what she was doing. When taken to a hospital, she maintained her manic behavior, constantly walking and talking, even though she was heavily drugged. Several days later, she was quiet, withdrawn, and very depressed.

Manic behavior can be a cover to hide underlying depression. Behind the manic mask is a depressed person. Manic persons unconsciously know that as long as they are talking, we cannot speak to them; as long as they hide, we cannot see them; as long as they are crazy, we will withdraw. To see with compassion the person hiding behind the manic mask is the therapeutic challenge.

We can also become psychotic in the involutional stage of life. Although these persons have usually never been psychotic, in middle age they are overwhelmed with worry, anxiety, frustration and sometimes feel that everyone is against them. Seemingly for no reason these persons feel so awful that living is an overwhelming burden. Even though they have functioned normally throughout life, they suddenly feel helpless or listless in coping with life. Although life basically made sense, now nothing makes sense.

Think of this fifty-six-year-old woman. She had always been

very active in raising four children and in being involved in various activities. She found herself so despondent that she had no energy or desire to do housework, get out of the house, or even converse. Out of concern, her children and husband agreed to electric convulsive treatment. After nine treatments she felt less depressed but in several months she was incapacitated again, and after another series of shock, she was taken to a different doctor. In the first session, this woman found that she had much to be depressed about. She had practiced motherism to a high degree and since her children were no longer with her, she felt lost and useless. Furthermore, her husband was a workaholic. She hardly knew him and felt some resentment toward him. Social activities no longer appealed to her; they seemed to be escapes from the real issues of her situation. And her family, with good intentions, tried to force her to be her "old self," which was impossible and not the best for her. Still, she felt guilty and more depressed for letting her family down, and she repressed her anger at them for letting her down. By experiencing her limits and re-evaluating her life, she came to new meaning, and by loving her as she was, the family helped her to accept herself instead of her feeling guilty. Her unhealthy mode of living helped her to find and live a better life.

It is not rare to see a middle-aged person questioning the meaning of life, judging oneself as quite limited and worthless, and doubting the love for and from those close to them. To feel guilty or resentful about the past or to feel angry about the past and present are not uncommon. To see a meaningless future and to feel helpless about it can reach psychotic proportions. Death may seem to be the only meaningful answer. Yet journeying in the valley of death can bring a new appreciation of life. The spirit is often rekindled in the desert.

HOW WE CAN JUDGE THEM

How do we (normals) judge them (abnormals)? We may assume that we know what mental illness is, what causes it, and what the prescribed treatment should be. But do we really know? Or, what do we know? Let us question some of our assumptions.

Some of our standards for judging mental illness, particularly psychosis, often include the following assumptions. Consensual validation is considered truth: If most of us think something is mad, then it must be mad—senseless or never as meaningful as our (normal) experience. But we have seen that when we are in the same formation and moving in the same direction, we may nevertheless be on a mad course. Our normal mode of living can be less authentic and more mad than their abnormal way.

Another assumption is the more formal education we have, the more qualified we are to judge. The medical doctor is normally seen as the person who is most educated and qualified to judge the presence or absence of mental illness, and the psychiatrist and neurologist are considered the physicians that can make the ultimate judgment. Although other people like psychiatric aides, nurses, social workers, psychologists, and other paramedical staff may also be qualified to make significant contributions and decisions, their truth is usually seen as secondary. Perhaps more important, though the patients have the inside story, they are seldom taken seriously. The assumption is that mentally ill persons are not qualified to make sense of their own lives.

Many of us, professional and non-professional, assume attitudes toward mental illness that can be but are seldom questioned. For example, one theory states that mental illness is basically the same as physical illness. The doctor makes a diagnosis on the basis of how the patient looks, functions, and feels—on signs and symptoms, and prescribes physical treatment. Yet, we do not know what exactly causes mental illness, and we do know that physical treatment only ameliorates symptoms. Seeing mental illness as a disease, we make assumptions that mental illness is not an experience that can make sense. We can deny that mental illness can include spirituality, or it can lead to a spiritual breakthrough. In containing or purging mental illness, we can block spiritual growth.

Some of us like to believe that mental illness is a disease like diabetes or the flu, especially if a family member is mentally ill. But there are differences between "being" mentally ill and "having" a physical disease. This does not mean that mental and physical illness are separate, but they are distinct. If we assume that they are identical, we can play normally mad games. For instance, we can think that we have little or no responsibility if mental illness is the same as having a physical disease. If a schizophrenic has a disease, then the family and the schizophrenic have little to do with it so that he or she should go to a doctor and be cured. If mental illness, however, is a way of being in the world—a mode of living, then we may have something to do with the way he or she lives. But we might prefer to hide the reality of mental illness by numbing "it," hiding "it," or by calling "it" a disease rather than admit that we may be part of the process.

For example, we can see schizophrenic persons as sick, crazy, childish, or enigmatic. Whatever the view, "we" have had nothing to do with "it" (them). We are afraid to admit that part of their madness may be our madness, that basically, unlike a disease, we can have plenty to do with mentally ill persons. Yet we do not listen to the sense of abnormal madness because listening might mean we are in it together. "Their" mental illness might be an indictment on "our" madness. Their dis-ease might be centered on our lack of spirit—on our ill-at-ease.

Mental health professionals and lay people often assume that it is nonsense to listen to and learn from the sense of mental illness. To see mental illness as a strategy or as a way of coping with normal madness is ridiculous in light of the above disease-entity model. Still, abnormal madness, like normal madness, can make positive and negative sense. We have seen that mental illness can be seen as a breakdawn of normal functions that can lead to a re-evaluation of life and eventually to integral living. To be sure, negative sense is also present in not being able to cope with everyday living, in minimizing freedom, and in suffering more or less unnecessarily. The sense, however, along with the nonsense should be understood and acted upon.

Another similar example of a possibly mad model is that mental illness is a "cause" of abnormal behavior. People act abnormally because they have a mental illness—as if they have a virus. Consequently, the patient, family, and society may take no responsibility for and make no sense of the experience. And the doctor may be willing to take the responsibility and try to tranquilize and "purge" the cause of this strange behavior. For instance, the patient tells the doctor that he feels depressed, and the doctor conveys to the patient that "a depression" is causing his illness. The doctor then prescribes drugs or electric shock to get rid of the cause so the patient can return to normal. The patient and family may feel relieved by thinking nothing is wrong with them, and the doctor may feel relieved for being in control.

Although some forms of mental disorders are organically caused, the mentally ill person is still a person whose experience is human and meaningful. We, however, like to blame mental illness as the cause of disruption, not that the person is disruptive perhaps for good reason. We fail to listen to the sense and nonsense of abnormal experience. We try to get rid of the "disease" and consequently expunge parts of people instead of learning from their abnormal experience.

Many of us simply see abnormal madness as a breakdown that cannot be a breakthrough. Like broken bodies or machines, people must be repaired to function normally again. But what happens if a psychotic person does not want to be normal and mad? What if madness is a dignified defense and protest against the pain inflicted by normal and mad people? We can fail to realize that mental illness can be a purgation of normal madness and a move toward mental health. Mental illness may involve a struggle for healthy love.

HOW WE CAN NEED AND TREAT THEM

To say that we (normals) may need them (abnormals) may also sound mad. For instance, too many normal people define themselves in terms of what they are not—like "them." We assume that if we are not abnormally mad—crazy, then we are healthy. We have seen, however, that we can prevent mental illness, be normal, and still be mad. We can also use abnormally mad people to serve as scapegoats. As long as abnormally mad people exist, we can feel there are some people who are lower and sicker than we—and, we can feel higher and healthier than they. At least, "we" are not like "them." This is also a mad illusion of normality.

Furthermore, we might feel we cannot afford to have many abnormally mad people become healthy and return to society. What would happen if ninety percent of mental hospitals were closed—if "we" would accept "them" or if there were no we-them dichotomy, but only people struggling together? It is possible that far less people would be institutionalized if we accepted and cared for them as being with us. But we would have to give up our precarious security that is based on a mad sense of superiority and health.

Indeed, abnormally mad people do differ from us: They more or less cause and have difficulty living in normal society; they hurt abnormally; most of them are socially ostracized; and unlike us, they are usually not accepted, sanctioned, or trusted. When they sufficiently disturb us, we label and more or less ostracize them. To return to normal formation, they must show significant change from abnormal to normal behavior. This process of "normalization" often involves much normal and mad pressure.

Consider a psychiatric hospital—a place where abnormally mad persons are treated to return to normal society. Madness in the name of mental health can occur when we expect them (abnormally mad people) to conform to our normal madness. Although some psychotic persons may be better persons and relatively happier than us, (we) the normal staff can pressure them to be like us—spiritually worse and unhappier. Patients can be pressured to replace their abnormal madness with normal madness, even though one of the reasons they are abnormally mad may be to escape from normal madness.

Games can be played between them and us. For instance,

abnormally mad persons may have to admit to madness, pretend
that the staff is right, and begin to look like and act as the staff.
And, they may learn to play the game of being normal: manifest
signs and symptoms of normal behavior, meet staff expectations,
and answer questions properly. For example, they may learn to
smile when depressed, to answer voices in private, to feign sleep
when awake. When they are interviewed to leave the hospital, the
games often continue and involve collusion. A doctor might ask
a patient: "You don't hear voices anymore, do you?" And the
patient responds "No, doctor, certainly not." "Do you feel
better?" "Yes, doctor, much better." The doctor may ask the
patient how he or she feels better and the patient says, "I don't
hear voices; I'm not anxious; I'm ready to lead a normal life."
When asked, the staff says the patient has been "good," which
often means the patient followed orders, asked no embarrassing
questions, and caused no disruptions; in short, the patient was not
a management problem.

Doctors, staff, and patient can enter into collusion— the doctor
and staff pretend that the patient is well, and the patient pretends
that the doctor and staff are not pretending. The point is that
patients can easily hide their true and mad self behind a facade
of normal madness that satisfies the mad staff. Too easily, the
normally mad staff can pressure abnormally mad patients to be
like them—normally mad. How patients really feel is seldom
pursued. When patients promise to continue to act normally,
they are cautiously allowed to re-enter normal formation.

Persons often hide unhealthiness because of the difficulties
of expressing and learning from abnormal madness. Madness as a
meaningful mode of communication is seldom considered, and
madness as a potential growth experience is often judged hereti-
cal. To be honestly mad in a madhouse can be difficult. The goal—
to exercise madness via physical and psychological treatment—often means not to listen to and learn from madness. Feeling guilty
and embarrassed about themselves, many, though not all, mad

people succumb to the mad pressure of playing the game of being normal.

We normals also tend to lump abnormal people into one category, making them all the same. We may see abnormal people as having no individual differences like ourselves. The point is that all mad people are unique. Labeling them all the same can enable us to treat and control unjustly their significant and often threatening experiences. Instead of respecting people and understanding their unique worlds, we can use the same method on everyone as if everyone were the same. Instead of extending ourselves, we can keep a safe distance from them. Labeling can be an official proclamation of the manufactured differences between us and them.

Actually, the similarities between us and them are far greater than the differences. Normal and abnormal people are quite alike: We all stand on the same ground, breathe the same air, really want much the same, seek the same sense. Thoughts, feelings, values and experiences are more alike than dissimilar. Still, we are afraid to risk ourselves: to step into the unknown, to listen to the uncanny, to see the bizarre, to touch the depth of being mentally ill. We hide behind our mad masks of mental health.

We often have the power to treat them almost as we wish. If a person is schizophrenic, then tranquilizers can be administered. If a person is depressed, electric shock treatment may be recommended. If a person is uncooperative, solitary confinement is encouraged. Think of the 21-year-old patient who was put in solitary confinement for threatening to punch an elderly patient. The hospital chart stated that the patient showed inappropriate and potentially dangerous behavior. When asked the following day what happened, the young man said that he wanted some solitude, but knew that the staff would deny his request and call it crazy. Consequently, he did something "crazy," threatened the old man whom he never intended to harm.

Although we think we can control most of their actions, our

control can be an illusion. The fact is that "they"—abnormal people—still live their own lives. Although many rights, opportunities, and power can be taken from them, they can still with ingenuity think their own thoughts, feel their own feelings, and make some sense of madness. For instance, hospital patients may intentionally and spontaneously build a covert communcation system in and outside the hospital. When a new patient or doctor arrives, the news is quickly passed around, or when the staff is considering a new program, the patients often know before they are told.

Abnormal mad people manage to keep their dignity. Despite the lack of respect and the bribes to be normal, they preserve a sense of personal worth and sometimes can make fools of the staff. A 27-year-old schizophrenic woman put it this way: "If you don't act crazy, they will think they taught you a lesson and expect you to be docilely grateful. The staff tells you why you're sick and how to get better, and then takes credit for your so-called recovery. You have to be the way they want you to be. Why should I let them do that to me? I have to keep some of my dignity."

Nevertheless, abnormally mad people can be exploited. In our urge to cure deviance, we can unjustly practice on people already defined as deviant. We have or take the power to test our methods on them—the powerless. The powerless can be "expendable" members of the population—abnormals like criminals, psychotic patients, sexoffenders, and hyperactive children. For example, they can be used in questionable experiments or research projects for which few of us would volunteer. Abnormally mad persons can be urged or bribed to volunteer for an experiment by promising them privileges that they would otherwise not get. Or the researcher might explain the project ambiguously to give an illusion of expected improvement.

Electric convulsive treatment, for example, was originally used on schizophrenic patients because the researchers thought that schizophrenia and epilepsy were mutually exclusive. Since ECT induces convulsions similar to those of grand mal epilepsy, we thought that ECT might cure schizophrenia. We discovered that our hypothesis was false but found that ECT can ameliorate depression. How much choice did the patients have, and how much real choice do they have now? Are the possible side effects honestly explained and considered? Like drugs, ECT can lessen depression and stress and can enable people to cope better; these changes, however, are often temporary. And what do these people learn from their being depressed or anxious?

Another form of normal madness is to administer drugs simply to control and manage patients. To be sure, drugs and ECT can be useful to lessen pain and symptoms that impede normal living. Instead of becoming drug dependent and leading semi-normal and chemical existences, we can see drugs as temporary means to help us cope better. We should, however, eventually try to understand what our experiences may mean or may be saying about our lives. A danger is to use drugs to numb experiences that may lead to or be part of spiritual growth. We can impede spirituality in our mad attempts to maintain normality. Here, drugs can often be used for the benefit of the staff (for better management) rather than for the therapeutic (whole) welfare of patients. Of course, the staff can say that drugs are given for the "good" of the patient.

Psychosurgery may be the most controversial physical treatment. The original method of cutting into the frontal brain lobes to change behavior, especially "abnormal aggression," has been replaced with modern techniques like placing lesions in the limbic system (the emotion-controlling portions of the brain) or using ultra sound, electricity, and tissue freezing. Still, many people question the ethics, effects (like possible loss of creativity and of certain intellectual functions), and the experimental nature of such brain tampering.

Another mode of treatment is behaviorial therapy. Consider a token economy program where patients must act in certain ways to get tokens that buy necessities and privileges like a mattress, three meals a day, and ground "privileges." When patients manifest the expected behavior, they are given a token and that behavior is reinforced. Basically the theory states that people are more likely to respond in ways that are rewarded and abstain from behavior that is punished. When given humanly and honestly, such programs can help people learn discipline and basic behavior patterns. But when psychologists are inhuman and dishonest, they serve the scientific madness of the researchers more than the therapeutic welfare of patients. Even though many patients see through such games, they can still be treated as less than human. As many people say: "They are like children." The fact is that they are not like children but are more like us.

Why do people who run unjust programs seldom take the same approach with their own families? Granted, the "therapist" will say that his family is not sick; however, the researcher makes the assumption that because people are sick they are essentially different. The therapist would not give his or her spouse tokens because he or she showed socially acceptable behavior, but may feel no qualms in giving them to a mentally ill person.

Or think about how we decide for them what is acceptable or unacceptable behavior. Do we have the right to decide for them? Can we decide? For example, when a schizophrenic patient mentioned that a nurse had attractive legs, the psychologist reinforced him negatively by taking tokens from him. When another psychologist questioned this decision, the therapist said it was obvious that the patient's behavior was unacceptable. Perhaps what was obvious was that the therapist had more problems in this area than the patient.

Many of us are afraid to listen to abnormal experiences in ourselves and in others. Perhaps we feel that listening may evoke our own abnormality and indict our normality. Those of us who dread the critique and call of abnormality are likely to control and numb abnormal experiences via "treatment" that helps us feel secure in handling the patient. As pointed out, psychotic people can acutely criticize normal madness and make us feel uneasy.

Madness, both normal and abnormal, can make little sense to normal people. Of course, this is a form of normal madness.

CONCLUDING REMARKS

Abnormally mad persons usually do not like being unhealthy but they often feel helpless to change. Although they may be well-intentioned, they feel compelled to be and act the same way. Still, their pain can mean that they want to be healthy and can be more than they are. Ideally, when they accept and learn from their experiences and behavior, they can become more fully themselves. Still, unhealthy persons often need help. For instance, by accepting and understanding mad persons, we can encourage them to accept, understand, and appreciate themselves. Our unconditional concern is therapeutic—it increases their well being. Or a qualified professional may be needed. Both friends and therapists help unhealthy persons to discover themselves. We should not identify them with their problems, but see them as persons who are infinitely more than their "problems." We can strive to be genuinely compassionate to care for them as one of "us."

All psychotic people are human beings, persons who make sense and who are worthy of respect. They primarily deserve the presence of people not the techniques of treatment. This does not mean that if psychotic persons are loved they will become healthy; it only means that their psychotic experience will be humanized. Treatment (psychological and physical) is also important and helpful when it is an implementation of care. Care without treatment is spiritual fantasy—and, treatment without care is scientific barbarism.

To love and treat them as ourselves, however, does not mean to treat them as if they were made of glass—to overcompensate for them or to excuse them from active responsibility. Madness is usually no excuse for irresponsibility or for badness, nor does it usually exclude or excuse individuals from leading meaningful lives. Mad people should be cared for and treated essentially the same as healthy people. Within the context of genuine care and technique, there is no guarantee, but there is hope that both abnormal and normal people will come to healthiness. All of us—normal and abnormal—are struggling together to find permanent meaning. When we admit and affirm our common ground, the more likely we are to emerge from mad to healthy and happy living.

Chapter Eight

Beyond Normality

Many assumptions about normality, health, and madness have been questioned and perhaps modified. To assume that normality and health are synonymous can be self-deceptive and harmful. To identify people with their physical, psychological, and social dimensions can fragment and violate them. To consider madness as only an abnormality can be a normal and mad judgment that violates both normal and abnormal people. Since many normal assumptions have been challenged, a summary explanation of my assumptions and a brief statement on psychospiritual health will be offered.

To be healthy is an ideal. Psychospiritual health is not a goal or state that one day is perfectly achieved, but it is an ideal that is imperfectly but perpetually realized. The contention is that the measure of a person depends primarily on the struggle to actualize these ideals, not only on the results. What or who are we, and how and why do we live when we are healthy?

When healthy, we are both normal and abnormal. We maintain and actualize ourselves to the fullest possible degree without madness. We are normal: Satisfying basic needs, adjusting to reality, and coping with the vicissitudes of living give security and contentment. And though we are not mad—abnormally or normally, we are abnormal.

We go beyond normality and do far more than simply live a life of maintenance and adjustment. Experiencing more than is minimally required, we burst out of normal formation and take the risk of being a bit weird. Along with being psychologically adjusted we consistently actualize our spiritual potentialities. We realize that being healthy—growth in integral living—incorporates spirituality as the paramount dynamic. Thus, we take care to foster spiritual growth as well as our psychosocial and sexual growth. We have the courage to be a bit different—to be healthy.

Instead of automatically being programmed with and by cultural madness or unconsciously following mad scripts, we can face, accept, and make sense of the culture and people, listen to our own rhythms, and write our own scripts. To be healthy, we have one foot in normal formation and one foot out. We are with and for others and are uniquely ourselves. We can realize that normality and abnormality exclusive of each other are forms of madness. Instead of being totally in the culture, we can encounter the culture.

As healthy people, we see better than normal or abnormal people. In constantly expanding our vision, we experience more of reality, deepen truth, trust and believe in what we see, and act on our sight. Instead of being locked into one approach, we are free to take a stand based on how we see the truth and on what we think is best for the situation, not simply for ourselves. What is best for the situation—which includes ourselves, near and remote others, and past, present and future experiences and standards—is a basic principle for judgment and action. We are careful not to block out reality or to deceive ourselves as madmen do or have gaps in our personalities that are filled with fantasies and anxieties, but our expanding vision of ourselves, others, and the world liberates us from madness and for health.

Concretely, we are contemplative. We see life in love. Transcending categorical and analytical thinking, we actually see more of reality—quantitatively and qualitatively. We can experience the interrelatedness of everything and of everyone—that we are all manifestations of humankind. Going beyond such mediation as thought, neediness, and goals, we can be purely present in love. Such a loving posture radically opens horizons of meaning.

Instead of selective attention—hearing only what fits our framework—we can hear and listen to reality more openly than mad people. We are basically open people who constantly change and deepen our points of view. Realizing that no one speaks about nothing, we try to listen to and act on the sense and nonsense in others. We also listen to ourselves—feelings, thoughts, values— make a decision, and act the best we can. We are searching people who are willing to expand our world and in fact expand all our senses. We realize how the senses of taste, touch, and smell can put us in intimate contact with reality and how easy it is to be seduced by and to manipulate reality in the distal senses of seeing and hearing.

An availability to the truth of feelings also exists. Feelings are in immediate contact with reality and therefore seldom lie, but they are also ambiguous and ambivalent. We try to listen to what feelings say about ourselves and others. Having a creative control of feelings, we do not repress or minimize them as think-aholics nor do we overestimate the value of feelings as advocates of feelism. Rather, we are temperate persons who value the truth of feelings along with the truth of thought and inspiration.

A high degree of self-acceptance enables us to admit what is happening within and around us. We spontaneously embrace life as it emerges. Problems and feelings are not automatically pre-judged, but are considered appeals to listen more intently. For instance, when we feel depressed, we affirm, listen to, and some-times find explicit sense in our depression. Even if no overt mean-ing emerges, we let ourselves be depressed and save time and energy by not fighting ourselves. Eventually, we emerge out of our depression usually renewed.

We do not assume that such experiences as depression, anxiety, and loneliness are symptoms of or threats to psychological adjustment. Going beyond this view, we know that such experiences can be necessary parts of spiritual growth. Instead of identifying experiences with or interpreting them only in light of physical, psychological and social processes, we are also open to spiritual processes and meaning.

Healthiness means that we can let go and be with ourselves, others, and reality. Rather than compulsively manipulating, constantly ruminating, or being impulsive or hysterical, we can willingly let go and celebrate reality. Instead of being overly concerned with status or needs, we are capable of being unconditionally concerned with and for others.

Depending on the situation, we can be detached or involved. We are unlikely to be blinded by anxiety, threats, or rigid standards but are likely to face and cope with reality. We can enter significant and close relationships, though our lives do not absolutely depend on it. The odds are that we will formulate a few close and meaningful relationships with a sense of permanent commitment. Pledging ourselves to fulfill the call of love gives us significant direction, sense, and solidarity. Growing in the permanence of love is the essence and the ultimate force in our lives, and love makes us happy and good.

Solitude is a particularly fruitful way to keep in touch with self. Although thinking occurs in solitude, the time is basically for listening to and being in touch with self and others. In solitude, we affirm and deepen ourselves, judge and improve life, and strive for at-one-ment, re-collection, re-conciliation, and re-creation. Solitude is helpful in discovering and being ourselves in order to surrender to and for others.

Honesty is important in being healthy. We always strive to see and speak straight to ourselves, but not necessarily to others. This is not devious because we realize that honesty and sincerity are important avenues to truth, we are capable of keeping quiet or being "dishonest" in service of a higher truth. For example, when a true statement will harm rather than help another, we can abstain from speaking or say some other truth. We do not force people to see personal truth, but rather appeal to them. Seeing through the masks and beyond the periphery of people, we affirm the integrity and dignity of people. Instead of supporting interpersonal madness, we genuinely respect people for what they are and can become.

Creativity, integrity, and dignity are marks of healthiness. Our creativity is not necessarily expressed in the arts but always in self emergence. We are always on the way, perpetually realizing and opening up to new experiences. Instead of being normally static, we are constantly becoming.

Wholeness is not a goal to be achieved but a process to be perpetually realized. The on-going integration of our physical, psychosocial, and spiritual selves is a life-project. The crucial dynamic of normal madness is to defend against, forget, or minimize spirituality. The key dynamic of abnormal madness is physical and/or psychosocial malfunctioning. And as we have seen abnormal madness can be violated and normal madness can be reinforced. To be healthy—to grow in integrity—is to transcend both normal and abnormal madness.

In living the truth of wholeness we emerge with dignity. We come to experience a sense of worth that no one can take from us, for our worth lies in becoming wholly ourselves—not in craving things or success but in being wholly alive. Even if we are not satisfied or have never achieved success or if we have lost them, we still are worthwhile.

What makes life and us worthwhile is love. Love makes life come alive—a spirited life that no one on earth can give to or take away from us. And when no one accepts our love, we can still love life. Even when there is much to dislike and perhaps hate, there is always someone and something to love.

A refreshing sense of humor and play exists. We see funny things, the incongruent and unexpected. We can let go and laugh, can swing and dance with life. Instead of always trying to cope with and figure out reality, we get a kick out of living. And in many ways, play is seen as more important than work. To live and enjoy life as a mystery is more important than to cope with it as a problem.

To be healthy, we must be vigilant. We do not take life for granted. And the voice of death summons us to take care to live fully. We listen to and learn from our coming to death as well as the dying and death of others. Instead of denying death, we painfully celebrate it because we know that without death we cannot live. Being vigilant to the voice of death, we become lovers of life.

To be lovers of life we give for the sake of giving and care for the other's sake—not to get affirmation, respect, or recognition. We can also receive love and return the gift of ourselves. Instead of exploiting or seeing others as objects, we do what is best for them. Love is the core motivating force and ultimate concern of healthy people. We strive to love unconditionally—with no strings attached. Even when we are hurt in love, we struggle for the courage to stand in love and not withdraw or return the hurt. We know that in love we can accept and make sense of madness and badness—that a person need not be perfectly healthy or good to be loved. Love is the saving grace.

In love, we are redeemed and reconciled. The sacred and profane dimensions of our personality move more in concert. Instead of madly being at odds with life, we can celebrate and embrace life. We can become beautiful persons for whom life makes significant and permanent sense. We can become virtuous people.

To live lives of love we must be charitable. *Charity* is acting in love. As lovers we are free enough to choose and willing enough to act in love. Our charity means that we can and want to give to another in love. Charity is not the same as justice wherein we give the minimum demand of love. Charity means that we go out of our way for others. In this sense, charity incorporates sacrifice.

In charity, we may withhold a point of view because it may do more harm than good. Or we may do something for another, not so the other is indebted to us (a counterfeit of love), but because it helps the other. We give a person something not because we want someone to feel lower but because the person needs it. Our charity may also involve saying something that will hurt another but the hurt is in the service of the other's growth, not for our own satisfaction. Sometimes it is best to say "no" to a person.

Charity never makes anyone feel small. We can give to the so-called poor in the name of charity, but actually our giving is for ourselves, to make us feel better or to relieve past guilt feelings. This kind of charity is mad and only evokes resentment. True charity means that we go out of our way for another in such a way that the other person feels with and one of us.

Though charity can be expressed by giving things to the poor, such charity can involve little love and actually be more a matter of business or of enslavement. True charity is oriented more properly around our spirit, not around our materials. For this reason, charity may be needed much more in the suburbs than in the inner city, but the so-called rich like to give to the so-called poor. It makes us feel holy. Yet, who are the rich? Who are the poor? Who are happy? Who lives a life of love? Who is mad? Who is healthy? Who really needs help? The poor in spirit need much more charity. We too often have the sad and mad situation of the poor in spirit giving to the poor in things. This kind of "charity" too often promotes an alienation of people, not a community.

Being in love, we become faithful people. *Faith* is accepting in love. Being full of faith means that we can creatively accept what we do not understand, especially the mystery of love. Going beyond such madness as thinkism, powerism, and rationalism, we gratefully embrace people even though we do not understand them, and we are willing to admit and encourage experiences that we cannot explain or grasp. Our faith enables us to listen to the inexplicable voices of mystery and doubt—key forces in spiritual growth.

Our love makes us people of faith—a real witness to the incomprehensible, the mysterious, and the paradoxical. We do not act only when we are certain but our most fundamental actions are rooted in a more fundamental certitude. In fact, our option to love is rooted in faith. When we extend love to people, we are never certain what will happen. We give ourselves to others in faith. The paradox is that our faith promotes love, and love is the foundation of our faith.

In love we are full of hope. *Hope* is looking in love. As hopeful people we look beyond the everyday and seductive dimensions of madness to the transcendent. Rather than taking things for granted at their so-called face value, we look for the possibility of deeper meaning. And, in love, we usually find it. Instead of being content with what we have, we let life perpetually emerge, experiencing what we can possibly expect or can hope for. We go beyond satisfaction and success by waiting in love for the best to occur. This is not a wishy-washy stance, a passive acceptance in letting life take over. Hope is simply an affirmation that life is more than we can comprehend.

Loving people are also prudent. *Prudence* is thinking in love. As prudent persons we are not prone to be impetuous or prejudiced or to be advocates of feelism or thinkism. Thinking in love means we are more likely to make charitable and loving judgments that are best for the situation, for us, and for others. In love we are open to many perspectives, not merely to our own, and we can become reasonable persons who can be reasoned with and who can reason. Rather than being closed to other points of view that conflict with our own, we strive to listen and work things out.

Thinking in love makes it more probable that we will make the right decision. It is not guaranteed that we are always right, but we are more likely to think and learn from our mistakes. Since our love tends to keep our judgments in harmony with experience, we are likely to do what is best for the total situation. Thinking is not a mental masturbation, a way of simply satisfying our own needs or of making others think that we are intelligent. Thinking and decision making are ways of doing what we think is best.

Judgments of prudent people are apt to be just. Thinking in love makes us more capable of giving what is due in love. *Justice* means that we give at least the minimum of love in a situation, even though we usually transcend this justice. Though what is right is straight-forward, we realize that a straight-forward position often has many facets. It is seldom a matter of either/or, but includes many viewpoints. However, we always take a stand—the stand of love.

Standing in love is *fortitude*. We do not have to worry or even care about how to appear strong or how to maintain our ground when we stand in love. Standing in love spontaneously makes us strong and gives us a ground, that goes infinitely beyond the strength and status of normal madness. Our spiritual strength is quietly heard and felt, and therefore may intimidate people. We may even seem weird because we do not constantly have to impress people or be on top of them as a way of compensating for our underlying and mad weakness. Spiritual strength encourages unification, being with—an unconventional experience.

Temperance is controlling in love. The control in love is not the control of repression or denial, but love is the control based upon discipline to listen to and to follow the meaning of experience. In love, we control our thoughts, feelings, and behavior. We learn an internal discipline that we trust and that keeps us maturing.

Being temperant, we are open and flexible in our judgments. We are neither hysterically impetuous nor aggressively biased, but we can silently follow and firmly speak the truth as we hear it. Our affective life is also inclined to be in harmony with the truth of the situation. Rather than being explosive or implosive, we are tempered and in harmony with the rhythm of life. We are unlikely to be overly-aggressive or to lose our temper, and neither are we likely to become so dependent that anything is all right. And we seldom overindulge in or starve ourselves from the satisfactions and responsibilities of life. We are unlikely to fast or feast as ends in themselves. We know that fasting in itself is morbid and masochistic, and feasting without fasting is being spoiled and narcissistic. Yet we can and do fast in service of feasting. We find and live according to our temperament, which is guided by and rooted in love—the spirit of life. Our control in love is one of letting be and being with.

Wisdom is knowing in love. We have seen that spiritual knowledge goes beyond rationality to the transrational and transcendent. In love, our horizons never end. We see inexhaustible perspectives. We see life in light of eternity. Rather than being seduced by the present, fixated in the past, or programmed by the future, our presence is a project that creates a meaningful past.

We take a certain distance and a certain intimacy toward a situation. We can be distant enough to see things in proper perspective and not to become over-identified with the situation, and we can be close enough to know what is going on and to get a feel for the situation. Our respectful intimacy enables us to grow in wisdom.

Understanding is seeing in love. Such seeing is not seeing what we want or only what is congruent with our views. Seeing in love is basically understanding the other person's viewpoint. It does not necessarily mean that we condone other people's opinions, but we do understand them.

To see another's viewpoint, we temporarily give up or suspend our own viewpoint. Love gives us the willingness and the strength to do this, for we know that we will not lose our ground in giving up our views. By understanding others, we can help them to understand themselves. We can help them to broaden their viewpoints and be free. Seeing in love means that we go beyond ourselves.

Although we are usually not professionally prepared to do counseling, we can be consoling and therapeutic. *Counsel* is helping in love. Our love motivates us to want to help others and our wisdom and understanding enable us to implement our concern. Our loving stance enables us to ease suffering, to support others in stress, and in general to be with and for others. Our love is therapeutic in promoting the well-being of self and others.

Our counsel does not primarily depend on professional training or technical skills but is simply an implementation of our love. Indeed, competent education can help us to become better counselors or at least a certain type of counselor. However, we are talking about a type of counseling that is basic or possible to all people. In fact, some training can help us to forget our natural counseling talent and become mad professionals who are less consoling and helpful than non-professional people.

Affirming in love is *humility* and *pride*. In love we can affirm who we are and who others are. We serenely proclaim our transcendent spiritual selves. A proud "yes" to feeling one with the universe is tempered by a humble "yes" in knowing our place in the world. In love we are both proud and humble. Pride without humility is an egoistic and arrogant existence. Humility without pride leads to an inadequate and masochistic existence.

Authentic lovers are also reverent. *Reverence* is spontaneous awe and wonder in love. In love we approach one another with a certain trembling fascination, an uncanny attraction. We experience another as someone who is foreign and familiar, someone we know and do not know. We opt to plunge into the unknown land, and yet we feel we will be at home in love—a place where everyone can build, share, and enjoy.

We can deeply respect others without maudlin sentimentality or aggressive manipulation. We really can see another as a person of unequaled and priceless worth. We can affirm the other's dignity and validate their place. We let others feel lovable and loved no matter what.

A key characteristic of living is compassion. *Compassion* is suffering with in love. In love, we discover that all of us stand on the same ground, a ground of joy and pain. We spontaneously know what people feel and we have a feeling for them. We can intuit what they are going through, and love enables and encour-

ages us to suffer with them. We hope that others will be able
to transcend their pain and no longer suffer unnecessarily. Nevertheless, compassionate love enables both of us to come closer to
each other and to make sense of life's apparent nonsense.

Compassion means that we can extend ourselves to others, not
only in the comfortable times but also in the uncomfortable ones.
Rather than madly withdrawing from another in undesirable
moments, we may find ourselves even coming closer in these painful times. We experience another's suffering as an opportunity to
deepen our love and to acknowledge that we too are suffering
people. We are all wounded people in need of healing.

In love we are committed people. *Commitment* is standing for
others in love. As lovers we stand for something, not just temporarily, but forever. We grow throughout life in the permanence
of love. Love is not madly based on likes, comforts, qualities,
functions, this or that. All these qualities are temporary and dissipate with the passing of time. Committed persons have depth
and direction in living. Life can go far deeper than the surface
of normalcy and be more than a mad series of circular and repe-
titious motions. We discover that only in love can we experience
what we are looking for—something to hold on to forever. Love
is permanent.

Loving people are full of joy. *Joy* is playing in love. In joy
we celebrate being in love. We can celebrate by ourselves—we
can go out in the fields and sing of love or we can rest in solitude
and listen to love. He can also celebrate with others. We can
feast with and enjoy people. Our playing in love together becomes
a witness to a community of love.

Love makes us ultimately free. *Freedom* is determinating oneself in love. Our love enables us to determine ourselves and to
behave in accordance with authentic values. Although we may be
shackled with unhealthiness, we can still find fundamental meaning by loving. We are not apt to be seduced by the madness of
everyday living or by our own demons. Our loving is a liberating
force to determine ourselves and to transcend madness.

When healthy and/or holy, we are lovers of life and consequently good persons. *Goodness* is promoting life in love. We take care to grow in love daily—knowing that love must be nourished and nurtured to survive and grow. Perpetually growing in the permanence of love, we grow in completion and experience a sense in life that no one can take from us. No matter what, we can say "yes" to life. We are happy.

Happiness is living in love. Life makes sense even in the throes of non-sense. Even when under stress, we can experience a fundamental harmony with life that transcends madness. *Peace* is resting in love. In love we feel serenely at home in life. We find our place and pace in living love.

If we honestly and truthfully struggle to learn from and transcend madness, we will not necessarily find health but we can find happiness. If we strive to live a life of love, we can become good persons—and, goodness is the core of happiness. This does not mean that we will always experience pleasure, be content, and lack madness. This is normality and not necessarily happiness. We are happy when life ultimately makes sense. If we tried and gave our best in love and struggled to live fully for self and others, we will die happy. To die happy is to have lived in love.

Selected Bibliography

Allport, Gordon W. *The Individual and His Religion*. N. Y. The Macmillan Co., 1950.

Bateson, G., D. D. Jackson, J. Haley, J. Weakland. *"Toward a Theory of Schizophrenia."* Behavioral Science, I, 25L, 1956.

Berdyaev, Nicolas. *The Divine and the Human*. London: Geoffrey Bles, Ltd., 1949.

Castaneda, Carlos. *Journey to Ixtlan. The Lessons of Don Juan*. N. Y.: Simon and Schuster, 1972.

Eliade, M. *The Sacred and the Profane*. N. Y.: Harper Torch Books, 1959.

Elull, Jacques. *The Technological Society*. Trans. by John Wilkenson, N. Y.: Vintage Books, 1967.

Fisher, William. *Theories of Anxiety*. N. Y.: Harper and Row, 1970.

Foucault, Michel. *Madness and Civilization. A History of Insanity in the Age of Reason*. N. Y.: Vintage Books, 1965.

Frankl, Viktor E. *The Doctor and the Soul. An Introduction to Logo Therapy*. N. Y.: Alfred A. Knopf, 1955.

Freedman, Jonathon L., J. Merrill Carlsmith, David O. Sears. *Social Psychology*. Englewood Cliffs, N. J.: Prentice Hall, Inc., 1974.

Green, Hannah. *I Never Promised You a Rose Garden*. N. Y.: The American Library, 1964.

Greer, Germaine. *The Female Eunuch*. N. Y.: McGraw-Hill Book Company, 1971.

Goffman, Erving. *Relations in Public. Micro-studies of the Public Order*. N. Y.: Harper Colophon Books, 1971.

Goffman, Erving. *Asylums*. Garden City, N. Y.: Anchor Books, 1961.

Heidegger, Martin. *Being and Time*. Trans. by John Macquarril and Edward Robinson. N. Y.: Harper and Row, Inc. 1962.

Herzog, Arthur. *The B.S. Factor: The Theory and Technique of Faking It in America.* N. Y.: Simon and Schuster, 1973.

Johnston, William. *Silent Music. The Science of Meditation.* N. Y.: Harper and Row, 1974.

Johnston, William. (ed.) *The Cloud of Unknowing* and *The Book of Privy Counseling.* N. Y.: Doubleday, 1975.

Jung, C. G. *Modern Man in Seach of a Soul.* Trans. by C. F. Baynes, N.Y.: Harcourt, Brace & World, Inc., Harvest Books, 1955.

Kaplan, Bert (ed.). *The Inner World of Mental Illness.* N. Y.: Harper & Row, 1964.

Kesey, Ken. *One Flew Over the Cuckoo's Nest.* N. Y.: The New American Library, 1962.

Kittrie, Nicholas N. *The Right to be Different. Deviance and Enforced Therapy.* Baltimore: Penguin Books, Inc., 1971.

Kraft, William F. *The Search for the Holy.* Philadelphia: The Westminster Press, 1971.

Kraft, William F. *A Psychology of Nothingness.* Philadelphia: The Westminster Press, 1974.

Kwant, Remy G. *Encounter.* Trans. by Robert C. Adolfe. Pittsburgh: Duquesne University Press, 1968.

Laing, R. D. *The Divided Self: An Existential Study in Sanity and Madness.* Chicago: Quadrangle Books, 1960.

Laing, R. D. *The Self and Others. Further Studies in Sanity and Madness.* Chicago: Quadrangle Books, 1962.

Laing, R. D. *The Politics of Experience.* N. Y.: Pantheon Books, Inc., 1967.

Lefebvre, Henri. *Everyday Life in the Modern World.* Trans. by Sacha Rabinovitch. N. Y.: Harper Torch Books, 1968.

Lindbergh, Anne Morrow. *Gift from the Sea.* N. Y.: Vintage Books, 1965.

Lyons, Joseph. *Experience:An Introduction to Personal Psychology.* N. Y.: Harper and Row, 1973.

Luijpen, William. *Phenomenology and Atheism.* Pittsburgh: Duquesne University Press, 1964.

Mackay, Charles. *Extraordinary Popular Delusions and the Madness of Crowds.* Wills, Vermont: L. C. Page & Co., 1932.

Marcel, Gabriel. *Being and Having.* London: Deare Press, 1949.

Marcel, Gabriel. *Man Against Mass Society.* N. Y.: Henry Regnary Company, 1950.

Maslow, Abraham H. *Motivation and Personality*. Second Edition. N. Y.: Harper and Row, 1970.

Maslow, Abraham H. *Religion, Values, and Peak-Experiences*. Ohio: Ohio University Press, 1964.

Nouwen, Henri J. *The Wounded Healer: Ministry in Contemporary Society*. Garden City, N. Y.: Doubleday, 1972.

Rosen, George. *Madness in Society. Chapters in the Historical Sociology of Mental Illness*. N. Y.: Harper and Row, 1969.

Ruesch, J. *"The Tangential Response"* In Hoch and Zuben (eds.) *Psychopathology of Communication*. New York: Grune and Stratton, 1958.

Ruitenbeek, Hendrik M. (ed.) *Going Crazy. The Radical Therapy of R. D. Laing and Others*. N. Y.: Bantam Books, 1972.

Scheler, Max. *Man's Place in Nature*. Trans. by Hans Meyerhoff. N. Y.: The Noonday Press, 1961.

Searles, H. F. *"The Effort to Drive the Other Person Crazy—An Element in the Etiology and Psychotherapy of Schizophrenia,"* British Journal of Medical Psychology, 32, 1, 1959.

Straus, Erwin W. *Phenomenological Psychology*. N. Y.: Basic Books, Inc., Publishers, 1966.

Szasz, Thomas S. *The Manufacture of Madness, A Comparative Study of the Inquisition and the Mental Health Movement*. N. Y.: Harper and Row, 1970.

Szasz, Thomas S. *The Myth of Mental Illness*. Revised Edition. N. Y.: Harper and Row, 1974.

Teilhard de Chardin, Pierre. *The Divine Milieu*. N. Y.: Harper & Row, Publishers, Inc., 1966.

Toffler, Alvin. *Future Shock*. N. Y.: Bantam Books, 1971.

Traub, S. H. and Little, Craig B. (eds.) *Theories of Deviance*. Itasca, Illinois: F. E. Peacock Publisher, Inc., 1975.

Underhill, Evelyn. *Mysticism: A Study in the Nature and Development of Man's Spiritual Consciousness*. N. Y.: E. P. Dutton & Company, Inc., 1911.

Van den Berg, J. H. *A Different Existence*. Pittsburgh: Duquesne University Press, 1972.

Watts, Alan W. *Psychotherapy: East and West*. N. Y.: The New American Library, 1963.

An Interesting Thought

The publication you have just finished reading is part of the apostolic efforts of the Society of St. Paul of the American Province. A small, unique group of priests and brothers, the members of the Society of St. Paul propose to bring the message of Christ to men through the communications media while living the religious life.

If you know a young man who might be interested in learning more about our life and mission, ask him to contact the Vocation Office in care of the Society of St. Paul, Alba House Community, Canfield, Ohio 44406 (phone 216/533-5503). Full information will be sent without cost or obligation. You may be instrumental in helping a young man to find his vocation in life.
An interesting thought.